Alabama Crosswords

Dale Ratermann

BLUE RIVER PRESS

Blue River Press
Indianapolis, Indiana

Alabama Crosswords
Copyright © 2012 by Dale Ratermann
All rights reserved under International and Pan-American Copyright Conventions

No part of this book may be reproduced, stored in a database or other retrieval system, or transmitted in any form, by any means, including mechanical, photocopy, recording or otherwise, without the prior written permission of the publisher.

ISBN-13: 978-1-935628-21-7

Cover Design: Phil Velikan
Layout: MaryKay Hruskocy Scott, Candor Creative, LLC
Editor: David Ruiz del Vizo, MADA Writing Services
Photos: Alabama arriving at the 2011 Academy of Country Music Awards, cover & page 10: Helga Esteb / Shutterstock.com; State Capitol Building, cover & page 43: Henryk Sadura; Natural bridge hidden in the forests of northern Alabama, cover & page 62: Jason Patrick Ross; U.S. Space and Rocket Center, cover & page 68: Rob Hainer / Shutterstock.com; Gulf Shores, Alabama, cover & page 95: Darryl Vest / Shutterstock.com; Camellia japonica, page 144: Ana Marques / Shutterstock.com.
State Region Illustration: Paris Chrisopoulos
Back Cover Map: MapResources.com

Printed in the United States of America
10 9 8 7 6 5 4 3 2 1

Blue River Press
Distributed by Cardinal Publishers Group
Tom Doherty Company, Inc.
www.cardinalpub.com

For Wilbert and Ruth

TABLE OF CONTENTS

Introduction

Put simply, the state of Alabama is diverse. The people are as diverse as the landscape. And the rich history is as diverse as the 21st century lifestyle.

From Huntsville to Mobile. From the top of Mt. Cheaha to the Gulf of Mexico. And from peanut farms to fashion malls.

This book will explore the people, places and activities that have made Alabama the great state that it has been for centuries.

Each chapter is filled with puzzles and stories to test your knowledge of the Yellowhammer State. Hopefully, you will be entertained, amused and educated.

There are challenges for readers of all ages, whether you are a lifelong native or a recent transplant, an urban dweller or a country charmer.

Alabama is a wonderful place to explore. Hike the hills, sail the waterways, bike the country roads and wander the cities.

"Share the Wonder." Enjoy the journey.

Part I: Alabama People

Shown arriving at the 2011 Academy of Country Music Awards, cousins Randy Owen (right) and Teddy Gentry (center), along with Jeff Cook (left), formed the country music/southern rock/gospel/pop band Alabama in 1969. The group continues to perform and record and has had 30 No. 1 hits and sold more than 70 million records.

Actors

Alabama has been a hotbed for growing actors of note.

Among the most widely recognized is Jim Nabors. The Sylacauga native was Gomer Pyle on *The Andy Griffith Show* and the spinoff *Gomer Pyle, U.S.M.C.* A stretch of U.S. Highway 280 in Talladega County is named in his honor.

Nell Carter (Birmingham) won a Tony Award for her performance in the Broadway hit Ain't Misbehanvin', but is best remembered for her Emmy-winning role of on *Gimme a Break!*

Courteney Cox (Birmingham) was Monica on the long running TV series *Friends*, then starred as Jules on *Cougar Town*.

Kate Jackson (Birmingham) was an original *Charlie's Angels* and won awards for her work on *Scarecrow and Mrs. King*.

Wayne Rogers (Birmingham) was Trapper John on *M*A*S*H* and received a star on the Hollywood Walk of Fame in 2005.

Channing Tatum (Cullman) starred in *Magic Mike*, a 2012 flick roughly based on his experiences as a male stripper. He also starred in *Dear John, The Vow* and *21 Jump Street*.

Tallulah Bankhead (Huntsville) was known for her husky and sultry voice and starred in dozens of Broadway shows and Hollywood hits. An avid baseball fan, she once said: "There have been only two geniuses in the world, Willie Mays and Willie Shakespeare."

George Lindsey (Jasper) was Goober on *The Andy Griffith Show* and *Hee Haw*. He created the George Lindsey/UNA Film Festival that has taken place in Florence every year since 1998.

Mary Badham (Birmingham) received an Academy Award nomination in 1962 at the age of 10 for her portrayal of Scout in *To Kill a Mockingbird*. She was in just three other movies (and made guest appearances on two TV series). Instead of staying in show biz, Badham became an art restorer and college testing coordinator.

Other noted actors with Alabama roots include Pleasant Grove's R.G. Armstrong (who appeared in more than two dozen Western films), Birmingham's Amber Benson (known for her role of Tara on *Buffy the Vampire Slayer*), Anniston's Michael Biehn (of *Hill Street Blues* fame), Decatur's Lucas Black (known for his work on the TV series *American Gothic*), Montgomery's Brett Butler (of *Grace Under Fire*), Addison's Pat Buttram (who portrayed Mr. Haney on *Green Acres*), Huntsville's Julia Campbell (of *Romy and Michele's High School Reunion*), Montgomery's Hosea Chanchez (known for his recurring role on *For Your Love*), Uniontown's Tony Cox (a dwarf known for his performance in *Bad Santa*), Clay's Clayne Crawford (of *A Walk to Remember*), Birmingham's Ashley Crow (of *Heroes*), Huntsville's Felica Day (known for her role of Vi on *Buffy the Vampire Slayer*), Huntsville's Kim Dickens (of HBO's *Treme*) and Birmingham's Louise Fletcher (who played Nurse Ratched in *One Flew Over the Cuckoo's Nest*).

Also: Mobile's Annabelle Gurwitch (of TBS's *Dinner and a Movie*), Madison's Robert Hoffman (of *90210*), Jasper's Polly Holliday (who played Flo on *Alice*), Mobile's Cooper Huckabee (who was in *The Funhouse* and *Urban Cowboy*), Decatur's Dean Jones (who starred in several Disney films), Helena's Rebecca Luker (who has received three Tony Award nominations), Gadsden's Sunny Mabrey (who has had roles on *Desperate Housewives* and *Mad Men*), Fort Payne's Philip Ober (who was Gen. Stone on *I Dream of Jeannie*), Huntsville's Debby Ryan (of *The Suite Life on Deck*), Bessemer's Glenn Shadix (of *Beetlejuice*), Montgomery's Octavia Spencer (who won a Golden Globe Award for her work on *The Help*), Birmingham's Gail Strickland (who appeared on *M*A*S*H* and *Seinfeld*), Birmingham's Barret Swatek (of *10 Things I Hate About You*) and Mobile's Richard Tyson (who appeared in *Kindergarten Cop* and *There's Something About Mary*).

Townes Sudoku

Use logic to fill in the grid so every row, column and 2x3 box contains the letters T-O-W-N-E-S, in honor of Harry Townes. The actor was born in Huntsville and graduated from the University of Alabama. He was an accomplished Broadway performer before appearing on dozens of TV shows from *Bonanza* to *The Incredible Hulk*. Solution on page 146.

		T			S
		N		E	
T			N		O
N		W			E
	N		E		
W			S		

Jim Nabors Sudoku

Use logic to fill in the boxes so every row, column and 3x3 box contains the letters J-I-M-N-A-B-O-R-S, in honor of Jim Nabors. The comedic actor was born and raised in Sylacauga and best known for playing Gomer Pyle in *The Andy Griffith Show* and *Gomer Pyle, U.S.M.C.* Solution on page 146.

A			O		S			R
		I				J		
R	N						B	O
		R		B		A		
	S		M		N		O	
		O		A		S		
I	B						N	A
		M				I		
O			I		B			M

Actors Crossword

Solution on page 146.

Across

1. Pilfer from Pier 1
6. Bushelon Funeral Home weeper
11. "Vi" on *Buffy the Vampire Slayer* who was born in Huntsville
14. Welsh dog at Murphy Kennel
15. University of West Alabama cowboy sport
16. Abbeville HS Valedictorian's rank
17. Decorate
18. "I knew it all ___!"
19. Piedmont City School District grp.
20. Disastrous drop (2 wds.)
22. Birmingham Fencing Club weapons
24. Troy University Latin 101 word
25. Olde South Gumbo ingredient
27. *Andalusia Star News* revenue source
30. The center of Summit?
31. Cuts in half in a Jacksonville State University biology class
35. Midway between drunk and sober at Mason's Pub
37. A long time at the Geological Survey of Alabama
38. Alabama Dance Academy jump
39. Biblical twin
40. Alabama Cavalry mount
42. Shoe Carnival shoestring
43. NAPA Auto Parts battery fluid
44. Annoy
45. Academy Award winner Robards
46. Eyewear for Mr. Peanut
48. Marriott Shoals Hotel & ___
50. Phenix City winter hrs.
51. Curly cabbage at Bruno's Supermarkets
52. Nervous twitches
54. Scrub pots at Cafe Dupont
57. New Zealand's largest city
61. Yang's counterpart
62. Singsong syllables
65. Like a Foot Locker shoe
66. Alabama Senate roll-call vote
67. Downy duck
68. Musical work at Samford's Wright Center
69. *Friends* actress who was raised in Mountain Brook
70. Alabama Nature Center fowl pole
71. Homeless in downtown Birmingham

Down

1. Piggly Wiggly checkout action
2. Kind of list
3. Greek love god
4. See eye to eye
5. "Goober Pyle" portrayer who grew up in Jasper
6. Lusts for a Baskin-Robbins sundae
7. Part in a Pell City Players production
8. Mentone Wedding Chapel vow (2 wds.)
9. Father Goose's poetic "nightfall"
10. *M*A*S*H* actor who was born in Birmingham
11. Numbskull
12. Wind Creek Casino buy-in
13. Affirmative votes in the Alabama House of Representatives
21. Doctrine: Suffix
23. Spanish dish at Maestro 2300
25. Mobile Symphony woodwind
26. Warm-hearted
27. Mr. T's group
28. Mirrored ball at Prose & Palaver Vintage
29. European country
32. Terminate

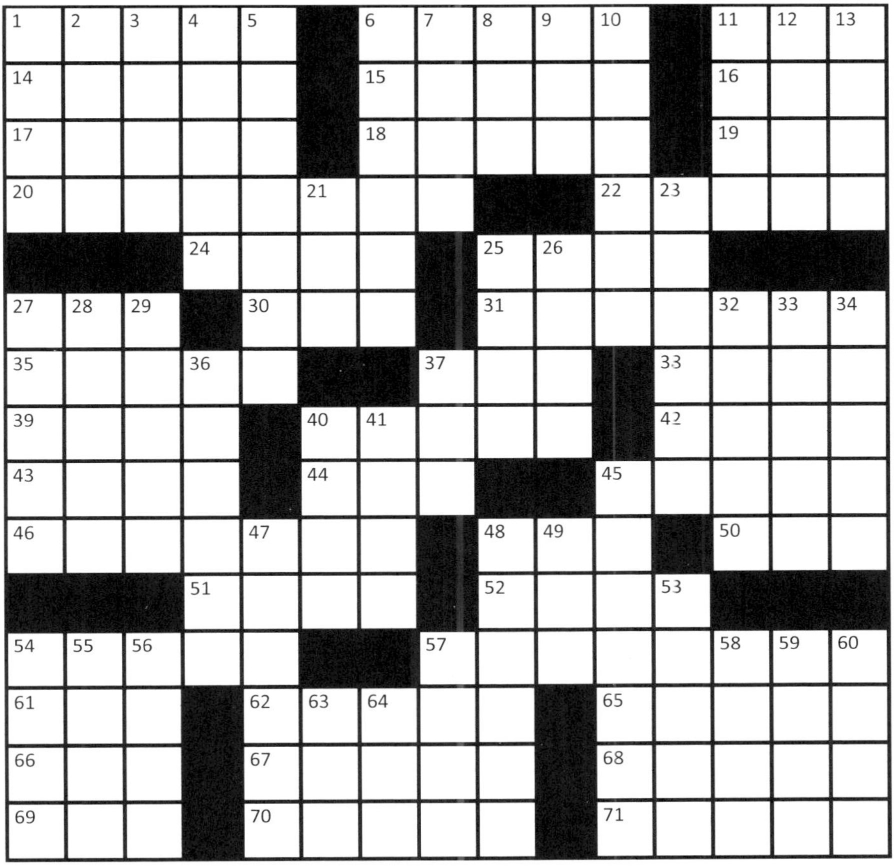

33. Snacks in shells at Rosie's Mexican Cantina
34. Used a credit card at Wal-Mart
36. *The Montgomery Advertiser* puzzle
37. *Gadsden Times* comics cry
40. Window part
41. Little River State Forest unit
45. One of the original *Charlie's Angels* stars who was born in Birmingham
47. Tony Award winner in *Ain't Misbehavin'* who was a Birmingham native
48. Oldest actress to be nominated for an Academy Award, Gloria ___ (for her role in *Titanic*)
49. *Alabama Magazine* photo, for short
53. Cloudmont Ski Resort run
54. In ___ (together)
55. Carrabba's Italian Grill good-bye
56. Black stone at Kay Jewelers
57. Port City Brewing beverages
58. Out of the wind on Lake Martin
59. Unlikely candidate for Carroll HS prom king
60. 6/6/44
63. 2016 Olympics city, briefly
64. *Much ___ About Nothing*

STUNT DOUBLES

The first and last names of 10 actors and actresses from Alabama have been split into two-letter segments. The letters in each segment are in order, but the segments have been mixed up. Put together the pieces in each line to come up with the performers' names. Answers on page 146.

1. CA SB LU CK LA ____________________
2. NS KE MD IC KI ____________________
3. TR AM PA UT TB ____________________
4. AY AD CI LI FE ____________________
5. BA DH MA AM RY ____________________
6. YC NE TE CO UR OX ____________________
7. SW EK AT RR BA ET ____________________
8. LY NG OU MI AE CH ____________________
9. MI LB HN CH IE AE ____________________
10. RI AR YS CH DT ON ____________________

Athletes

Some of the greatest athletes in the world have called Alabama home.

Jesse Owens was born in Oakville and went on to become one of the biggest stars in Olympic history. He won four gold medals at the 1936 Games in Berlin, dashing the hopes of Adolf Hitler to showcase Nazi Germany. Owens said the secret of his success was, "I let my feet spend as little time on the ground as possible. From the air, fast down, and from the ground, fast up."

Matching Owens with four gold medals in one Olympics (1984 in Los Angeles) was Carl Lewis. The Birmingham native won a total of 10 medals in four Olympic Games, including nine golds. *Sports Illustrated* named him the "Olympian of the Century".

Hank Aaron (Mobile) and Willie Mays (Westfield) are both considered among the five greatest baseball players in history.

Aaron set the Major League record for career home runs with 755 (later broken), appeared in a record 25 All-Star Games and was a two-time National League batting champion. He was inducted into the Baseball Hall of Fame in 1982.

Mays played in 24 All-Star Games and was a two-time National League Most Valuable Player. He was inducted into the Baseball Hall of Fame in 1979.

One of the greatest pitchers of all-time was Satchel Paige (Mobile). Relegated to the Negro Leagues for most of his career, Paige finally made his Major League debut at the age of 42. A statue of Paige was erected at the Baseball Hall of Fame in 2006.

Other baseball players from Alabama include Hall of Famers Ozzie Smith (Mobile), Billy Williams (Mobile), Willie McCovey (Mobile), Don Sutton (Clio), Monte Irvin (Columbia), Heinie Manush (Tuscumbia), Early Wynn (Hartford) and Joe Sewell (Mobile).

Joe Louis was born near Lafayette and spent 12 years in rural Alabama before his family moved to Detroit. He went on to become one of the best boxers in history. He won 66 of his 69 professional fights and became the Heavyweight Champion of the World in 1937 when he beat champ James J. Braddock. "The Brown Bomber" retained the title for 11 years, 8 months and 8 days, longer than anyone. The arena used by the Detroit Red Wings is named in his honor, he received a Congressional Gold Medal posthumously in 1982, and he was the first boxer whose image appeared on a U.S. postage stamp (in 1993).

Bo Jackson (Bessemer) is recognized as one of the greatest two-sport stars in history. He won the 1985 Heisman Trophy as the nation's top college football player and was selected No. 1 in the 1986 NFL Draft. He played in the NFL's 1990 Pro Bowl. As a baseball player, he was the Major League All-Star Game MVP (in 1989). He is remembered for his Nike commercials with the tag: Bo knows!

Alabama natives in the Pro Football Hall of Fame are Buck Buchanan (Gainesville), Ozzie Newsome (Muscle Shoals), John Stallworth (Tuscaloosa), Bart Starr (Montgomery) and Andre Tippett (Birmingham).

Top basketball players from Alabama include Charles Barkley (Leeds), Chuck Person (Brantley), Robert Horry (Andalusia) and Reggie King (Birmingham).

Golfers from Alabama who have won major championships are Larry Nelson (Fort Payne) who won the 1983 U.S. Open and 1981 and '87 PGA Championship and Stewart Cink (Huntsville) who won the 2009 British Open.

The top soccer player is Mia Hamm (Selma).

NASCAR's "Alabama Gang" set up shop in Hueytown and included Davey Allison (the 1992 Daytona 500 winner), Donnie Allison (a member of the International Motorsports Hall of Fame), Bobby Allison (a three-time Daytona 500 champion) and Red Farmer (named one of NASCAR's 50 Greatest Drivers).

UA or AU?

The University of Alabama and Auburn University have been home to some of the world's greatest athletes. Which school did these 10 athletes attend? (HINT: Five of them attended UA and five attended Auburn.) Answers on page 146.

	UA	AU
1. Golf pro Jerry Pate	☐	☐
2. Olympics sprinter Harvey Glance	☐	☐
3. Football quarterback Vince Dooley	☐	☐
4. Boxer-turned-governor George Wallace	☐	☐
5. Basketball star Robert Horry	☐	☐
6. Olympics sprinter Willie Smith	☐	☐
7. Football lineman John Hannah	☐	☐
8. Baseball all-star Frank Thomas	☐	☐
9. Football all-pro E.J. Junior	☐	☐
10. Olympics swimmer Rowdy Gaines	☐	☐

Athletes Crossword

Solution on page 146.

Across

1. "The Say Hey Kid" from Westfield
5. Catcher known as "Pig" from Bessemer who later served in the Alabama Legislature
10. Alexis' Exotic Body Art work, slangily
14. Border on, as Georgia
15. "Come here ___?"
16. Do damage to
17. Depend on
18. Assigned stars to
19. Black-and-white cookie at Kroger
20. Cheap accommodations at the Port of Mobile
22. South Seas attire
24. Crimson Tide tennis serving whiz
25. Talks wildly
26. Appetizer at Satterfield's Restaurant, maybe
30. Highest point, like the top of Cheaha Mountain
32. Koehler Cyber Cafe patron
33. Montgomery beauty shop
35. Birmingham-Shuttlesworth International Airport craft
38. Alabama puzzle theme and hint to 1-, 5-, 68- and 69-Across and 11- and 50-Down (2 wds.)
42. Downtown Mobile address abbr., often
43. Iranian money
44. Mobile Opera solo
45. Clothing
46. Alabama State Fair carnival pitchman
48. Jellied garnish
51. Gourmet Galley wine selection: Pinot ___
53. Divvies up
55. Nelson Stationers' supply (2 wds.)
60. Settled, as an Alabama Power bill
61. Pueblo brick
63. Alabama farm storage facility
64. Barely beat at Greenetrack
65. Rickey Smiley, for one
66. Marion Military, e.g. (Abbr.)
67. Auburn scholarship criterion
68. "The Wizard of Oz" shortstop from Mobile
69. Centerfielder on the Miracle Mets who hailed from Magnolia

Down

1. Neighbor of Earth
2. Aid in crime
3. Christmas in Dixie season
4. Taylor Eye Clinic affliction
5. Journalist Greeley
6. Can legally drink in Alabama (2 wds.)
7. Verbalize
8. "Didn't I tell you?"
9. Some Auburn linemen
10. Chest, in a UA anatomy class
11. "Hammerin' Hank" from Mobile
12. Sen. Lott
13. Birmingham pollutions
21. Frye CD section
23. Coleman Coliseum, e.g.
26. Havana's home
27. Quickly, in Energen memos
28. Geneva State Forest home

29. Athens State campus map blurb: "You ___ here"
30. Swiss peaks
31. Sessions or Bentley, briefly
33. Thick slice at Twin City Meats
34. Pledge of Allegiance ender
35. Yank
36. Cleveland's lake
37. Old Russian autocrat
39. Prop up
40. Big A Tires supply
41. Partner of pitch and roll
45. Prepared for action
46. Like state-of-the-art gadgetry at hhgregg
47. Dada artist represented at the Birmingham Museum of Art
48. Colorado resort
49. Relief from the sun
50. Mobile native who was the oldest rookie in the Major Leagues
51. One of the Judds
52. Elliptical path at the UA Observatory
54. Anatomical pouches
56. Where India is
57. Talladega engine knock
58. Ultimatum word
59. Learning method
62. ___ Perignon

ALABAMA ATHLETES HODGEPODGE

Find names in the categories listed, going up, down, sideways or diagonally in the letter grid. (Be careful; a name might fit into more than one category.) No letter is used more than once. When you have found all 21 items, there will be 39 unused letters. Start at the top of the grid, move from left to right and work down row by row, filling in the spaces provided with the unused letters to spell out a hidden message. Solution on page 147.

6 UA Football All-Americans

____

____

____

____

____

____

5 Auburn Football All-Americans

____

____

____

____

____

4 Alabama Baseball Hall of Famers

____

____

____

____

3 Auburn Basketball Stars

____

____

____

2 UA Basketball Stars

____

____

1 1936 Olympics Champion

____

R

O O S

G W T E S

E E W A T R T

R N C I A K I N G

S S N K B R E K C O R

W Y O N L T T E N N E B N

T E H E Y Y A E B R Y S O

I K R P E F E A T I D A S

S C H A L U O V R P O M K

S M E I K L N N O O C O C

T U N G R L A O G C N H A

M L L E A E M S O L C T J

A E L B R A R F T M M

R G I O T E U A R

G N V H P Y N

N E A S E

I M N

Y

Hidden Message:

___ ___ ___ ___ ___ ___ ___   ___ ___ ___ ___

___ ___ ___   ___ ___ ___   ___ ___ ___ ___ ___ ___ ___

___ ___ ___ ___   ___ ___ ___ ___

___ ___ ___ ___ ___ ___ ___.

Authors

Think "Alabama literature" and the first name to pop into most people's minds is Harper Lee.

The Monroeville native has published just one book in her life. But what a book it was: *To Kill a Mockingbird*. She won the 1961 Pulitzer Prize for Fiction and a Presidential Medal of Freedom for her classic work on race in America that was loosely based on her family and hometown in the 1930s.

Lee attended Huntingdon College and studied law at the University of Alabama. She wrote for college publications and was persuaded to write full-time. She spent two-and-a-half years writing the book, once tossing the uncompleted manuscript out the window in frustration.

One of Lee's childhood friends in Monroeville was Truman Capote, who wrote the acclaimed *In Cold Blood* (which Lee helped research). Other works by Capote included *Breakfast at Tiffany's* and *The Innocents*.

T.S. Stribling (Florence) won the 1933 Pulitzer Prize for Fiction for *The Store*. The novel was the second book in his Vaiden Trilogy, set in Florence and following three generations of an Alabama family.

Another Pulitzer Prize winning writer from Alabama is Rick Bragg. The Piedmont native won the award reporting on the Elian Gonzalez custody battle for *The New York Times*. His book, *All Over But the Shoutin*, deals with growing up in Alabama with an abusive alcoholic father.

Winston Groom's *Conversations with the Enemy* was a finalist for the 1983 Pulitzer Prize, but it took Tom Hanks to make Groom a famous novelist. Groom was living in Mobile in 1985 when he wrote *Forrest Gump*. The book was not a best seller. However, since Hanks starred in the 1994 film adaptation, the book has sold more than 1.7 million copies.

Other Alabama writers include: Asa Earl Carter (Anniston) who wrote *The Rebel Outlaw: Josey Wales* (under the alias Forrest Carter); Mark Childress (Monroeville) who wrote *Crazy in Alabama*, which was *The* (London) *Spectator*'s "Book of the Year"; Fannie Flagg (Birmingham), who wrote *Fried Green Tomatoes at the Whistle Stop Café* which was loosely based on the Irondale (Ala.) Café near Flagg's hometown; Gustav Hasford (Russellville) whose semi-autobiographical novel *The Short-Timers* was the basis of the Stanley Kubrick movie, *Full Metal Jacket*; Linda Howington (Gadsden), a.k.a. Linda Howard, who has published more than 60 romance/suspense novels and received the Career Achievement Award from the Romance Writers of America; and Bill Huie (Huntsville), who received death threats after publishing the novel, *The Klansman*, and had six books that were turned into movies.

Also: Zora Neale Hurston (Notasulga), who received a Guggenheim Fellowship to conduct research which led to the book *Their Eyes Were Watching God*, and co-wrote a play with Langston Hughes; Helen Keller (Tuscumbia) who wrote 20 books; William March (Mobile), who wrote the war novel *Company K* and was described by Alistair Cooke as "the most underrated of all contemporary American writers of fiction"; Robert McCammon (Birmingham), who has written more than 20 horror books, three of which reached *The New York Times* "Best Seller List"; Walker Percy (Birmingham) whose *The Moviegoer* won the National Book Award for Fiction; Sonia Sanchez (Birmingham), a poet who received a Pew Fellowships in the Arts; Mark Waid (Hueytown), an award-winning comic book writer; Daniel Wallace (Birmingham), who wrote *Big Fish: A Novel of Mythic Proportions*, which was adapted into a film by Tim Burton; and Tobias Wolff (Birmingham), who has won three O. Henry Awards for his short stories.

What's in a Name?

An anagram is a word, phrase or sentence formed by rearranging all the letters of another word, phrase or sentence. For example, an anagram for the name of Hueytown comic book writer MARK WAID is A WARM KID. Now match these Alabama writers with the anagrams listed. Answers on page 147.

1.	Albert Murray	a.	TOWING MORONS
2.	Margaret Walker	b.	PLAY WRECKER
3.	Winston Groom	c.	RED SILK CHARMS
4.	Walker Percy	d.	GANG LIFE FAN
5.	Fannie Flagg	e.	STEMWARE KIT
6.	Harper Lee	f.	REFER TRACTORS
7.	T.S. Stribling	g.	BRING STILTS
8.	Forrest Carter	h.	HEALER REP
9.	Mark Childress	i.	LARGE WATERMARK
10.	Mike Stewart	j.	MARRY A BUTLER

BONUS: Now it's your turn. See if you can create an anagram for Auburn grad-turned-novelist TIM DORSEY. There are no wrong answers. Our two-word anagram is what one might call a cheap novella.

TITLE BOX

Helen Keller's appropriately named autobiography was published in 1903. Starting with the large T in the shaded box, move one square up, down, left or right (but not diagonally) and continue to move that way to spell out the title of the book. The book's name runs continuously and uses each letter in the grid exactly once. Answer on page 147.

R	O	T	E
Y	**T**	S	F
O	H	E	I
F	M	Y	L

WILSON SUDOKU

Use logic to fill in the grid so every row, column and 2x3 box contains the letters W-I-L-S-O-N, in honor of E.O. Gibson. The Birmingham native won two Pulitzer Prizes in the General Non-Fiction category. Solution on page 147.

	I				
		S	N		
W		I	O		S
L		O	W		I
		N	L		
				W	

Authors Crossword

Solution on page 147.

Across

1. Slow down on I-10
6. No. on a HealthSouth business card
9. Kind of car or sandwich
13. "Calm down"
14. Huntsville Reproductive Medicine cells
15. Ruth's Chris steak sauce
16. In plain sight
17. Blend a drink at Red Star Tavern
18. Alabama State Fair barn females
19. Montgomery County courthouse event
21. *In Cold Blood* author who grew up in Monroeville
23. Massage locale
26. Perform for The Parable Players
27. To and ___
28. Shell gas station abbr.
29. Spanish appetizer
31. Birmingham Zoo eucalyptus eater
33. Word processing command
34. Oomph
36. Unlikely Outback Steakhouse patron
38. Birmingham author who won a National Book Award for *The Moviegoer*
39. Monroeville native who wrote *To Kill a Mockingbird*
40. Forrest Gump creator who lived in Mobile
44. Fire remnant
46. Nut job
47. Lascivious
50. Loosen, as laces
52. Highlander
53. Will Smith title role
54. Tigers bobblehead movement
55. Red Lobster kitchen meas.
57. It was dropped in the '60s
58. Birmingham native who wrote a Sarah Palin leadership book that reached *The New York Times* best-seller list
60. Kind of breath
62. A whole lot of 'Bama fans
63. Rank above maj. in the Alabama National Guard
64. Barely chewable
68. Works in the Birmingham Botanical Gardens
69. Israeli weapon
70. Word often preceded by poly-
71. Not straight
72. UAB Hospital employee, briefly
73. Film units at the Gulf Coast Exploreum IMAX

Down

1. Sis' sib
2. Gun an engine at Talladega Speedway
3. Downtown Pub brew
4. Miniature racer: Go-___
5. Uncredited actor in a South Alabama Film Festival flick
6. Shakey's Pizza ingredient
7. Wicked
8. West coast destination from BHM
9. Sirius Chocolate source
10. Alabama Adventure roller coaster feature
11. Like a brand new dress from Macy's
12. Beaten by the Tide
20. Gross
21. Rugged rock
22. Auburn psych class topic
23. Put one's foot down
24. Piece of glass at Window World of Montgomery
25. Mimicker

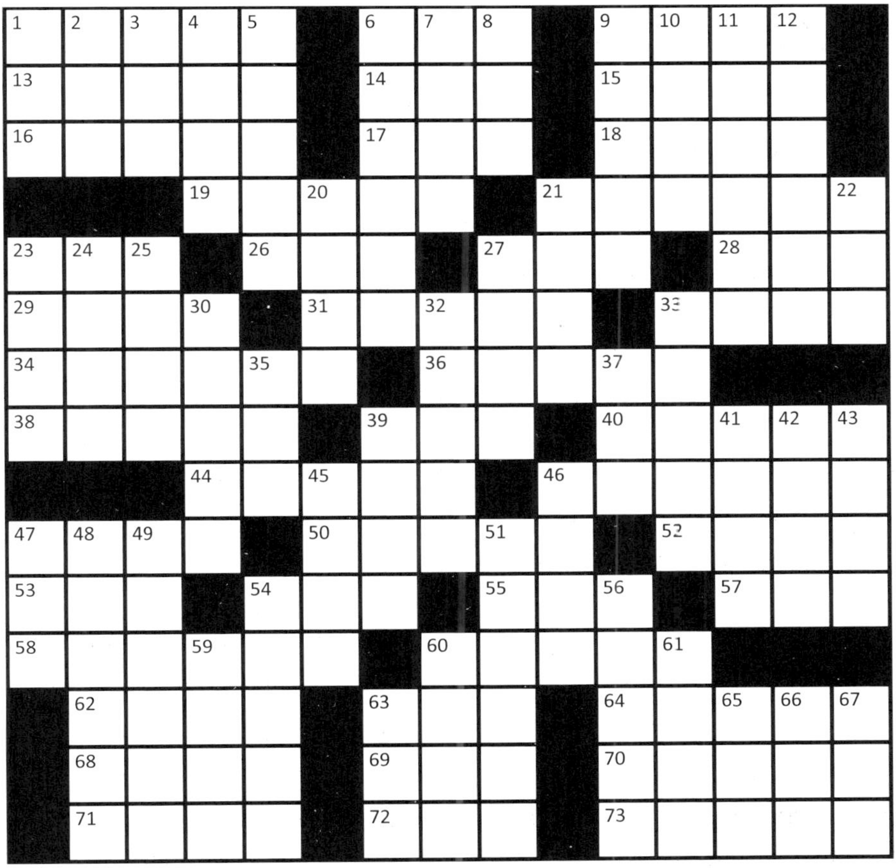

27. Run away from the Alabama Highway Patrol
30. Similar to a rainbow's shape
32. Ward off
33. Strip of equipment
35. Addison HS phys ed class
37. Put in storage at Braswell's Winery
39. Do PNC Bank work
41. Face-to-face exam at Oakwood University
42. Praiseful words from the Poet Laureate of Alabama
43. Jell-O former
45. Gulf channel marker
46. Left on an Alabama map
47. "Well, ___-di-dah!"
48. Actress Cuthbert
49. Weeping tree in the Macon State Forest
51. *Leaning* to the right?
54. Like Alabama A&M alumni magazine
56. Former Alabama governor, David ___ Lewis
59. Malicious look
60. Old TV clown
61. Baptist Health medicine amount
63. Something to chew on at Gilmer Dairy Farm
65. Western tribe
66. Classic Barber Shop goo
67. Selma Mall store posting: Abbr.

Industrialists

In 2011, Marguerite Harbert had a reported net worth of $1.2 billion, making her the richest person in Alabama. The 89-year old widow of construction company founder John Harbert ranked as the 355th richest person in the U.S.

After serving in the U.S. Army during World War II, Mr. Harbert graduated from Auburn University with a civil engineering degree. In 1949, he started his own construction business in Birmingham that grew into one of the largest in the country. He also had interests in mining, pipelines, land development and limestone quarrying. He died in 1995 at the age of 73.

Another construction titan was Winton "Red" Blount, a native of Union Springs. He founded his construction company in Montgomery in 1946. The firm worked on projects that included the Louisiana Superdome, Birmingham's First Avenue Viaduct and a Cape Canaveral complex that launched Apollo 11 to the moon.

Another Alabaman to hit it big in the business world is Tim Cook. The Robertsdale native is the CEO of Apple, succeeding the late Steve Jobs. He graduated from Auburn in 1982 with a degree in industrial engineering and earned his M.B.A. from Duke in 1988. Cook was working at Compaq in 1998 when Jobs convinced him to move to Apple.

Richard Scrushy of Selma was a high school dropout living in a trailer park when he returned to school. After earning a college degree from UAB, he started working in the healthcare industry and in 1984 founded HealthSouth Corporation, a global company with headquarters in Birmingham. But ethical and financial questions began to crop up in the 1990s. He eventually was convicted of 30 counts of money laundering, extortion, obstruction of justice, racketeering and bribery and is serving an 82-month prison sentence.

John Hendricks grew up in Huntsville and graduated from UA-Huntsville in 1974. He founded Discovery Channel in 1985 with $5 million in capital. Today, the company offers 28 network brands in more than 180 countries to more than 1.5 billion subscribers.

Stan O'Neal was born in Roanoke, worked on an automobile assembly line as a teenager and graduated from Kettering University. He wound up becoming President, Chief Executive Officer and Chairman of the Board of Merrill Lynch & Co.

David George Bronner earned a law degree from UA in 1971 and his Ph.D. in 1972. After serving as an assistant dean at the UA Law School, he became head of Retirement Systems of Alabama in 1973. The pension fund had $500 million in funds; today the fund has more than $32 billion in investments.

Anniston's Samuel Ginn graduated from Auburn in 1959 and became a pioneer in the wireless communications industry as CEO of Vodafone.

One of the greatest scientific minds in modern times spent 20 years working and living in Alabama. Wernher von Braun helped the U.S. win the race to the moon as the first director of the Marshall Space Flight Center at Redstone Arsenal in Huntsville.

George Washington Carver joined the faculty at Tuskegee Institute in 1896 and taught there for 47 years. His research helped improve farming, as well as find alternative uses for peanuts, sweet potatoes, soybeans, pecans and other crops. He urged farmers to rotate their cotton crops with other crops to improve the quality of the soil.

Another inventor from Alabama was Waldo Semon. The Demopolis native is credited with inventing vinyl, the world's second most used plastic. He made more than 5,000 other synthetic rubber compounds, held 116 patents and was inducted into the Invention Hall of Fame in 1995 at the age of 97.

Bama Holes

Fill in the missing letter for each of the words listed. Be careful, because each of the words can be completed with more than one letter. Transfer the correct letter to the corresponding blank so that the result is the name of a Hartselle native who is a former president and CEO of Time, Inc. Solution on page 148.

___ ___ ___   ___ ___ ___ ___ ___
1 2 3   4 5 6 7 8

1. _ONE
2. G_AD
3. CLA_
4. MO_T
5. _ATH
6. SA_E
7. COL_
8. I_CH

Drop Down Quote

The letters in each vertical column in the grid below go into the squares directly above them, but not necessarily in the order they appear. The black squares indicate the end of a word. When you have placed all the letters in their correct positions, you will have a quotation reading from left to right, row by row from Lonnie Johnson of Mobile who invented the Super Soaker water squirt gun. Solution on page 148.

				■					■			■			
								.	■				■		
				■										,	■
			■				■							■	
								.	■	■	■	■	■	■	■

A	A	D	E	I	E	E	C	E	R	I	H	E	I	N	D
I	F	D	S	R	H	E	M	F	T	I	M	E	S	S	M
I	L	E	T	S	L	N	S	K		O	S	N	S		S
L	M	E	Y		M	O	T			S	W				
O	N	F			S	U									

Industrialists Crossword

Solution on page 148.

Across

1. "Hell ___ no fury . . . "
5. Brawl
9. *The Taming of the* ___
14. Stellar Massage target
15. Fern Cave sound effect
16. Part of AWOL at Fort Rucker
17. Mister at the Schnitzel Ranch restaurant
18. Icy coating
19. Annoyed
20. Tone down
22. Like a requiem
24. Norwood Dental directive
26. Place for buoys and gulls
27. Purefoy Hotel's famous pie choice
30. Pack down
32. Coarse file
36. James Cameron 2009 blockbuster
38. East Alabama Paving goo
39. Spanish appetizer
40. Sessions or Shelby pos.
41. Toupee, slangily
43. Church of the Highlands bench
45. Go bad
46. Nose-in-the-air type
48. Lagoon Park Tennis Center match part
50. Appalachian bumpkins
52. Faulkner University science lab burner
53. Alternative drinks at Starbucks
55. Backside
56. House of Martial Arts discipline: ___ Chi
58. Cheapskate
60. Alabama ___ Commission
63. Graphite element
66. Early anesthetic
67. Pitch-black
69. Distinctive flair
71. Frighten at Popes Haunted Farm
72. Wranglers alternative at Macy's
73. Stride ___ Shoes
74. Birmingham Turf Club show place
75. Bingo relative at Creek Casino
76. Blow a horn for the Mobile Symphony

Down

1. "A likely story!"
2. High cards at the Mobile Bridge Center
3. Like most Madison streets
4. That lady's little demon? (2 wds.)
5. Air again on WBRC-TV
6. Least amiable
7. South Alabama Electric unit
8. Stocking stuffers
9. Snail trail
10. Framed basil? (2 wds.)
11. Ace Hardware garden tool
12. " . . . happily ___ after"
13. Marry
21. Iraqi currency
23. Alabama fish hawk
25. Have the corn chowder at Bonefish Grill
27. Out of fashion
28. Oak Mountain Amphitheatre affair

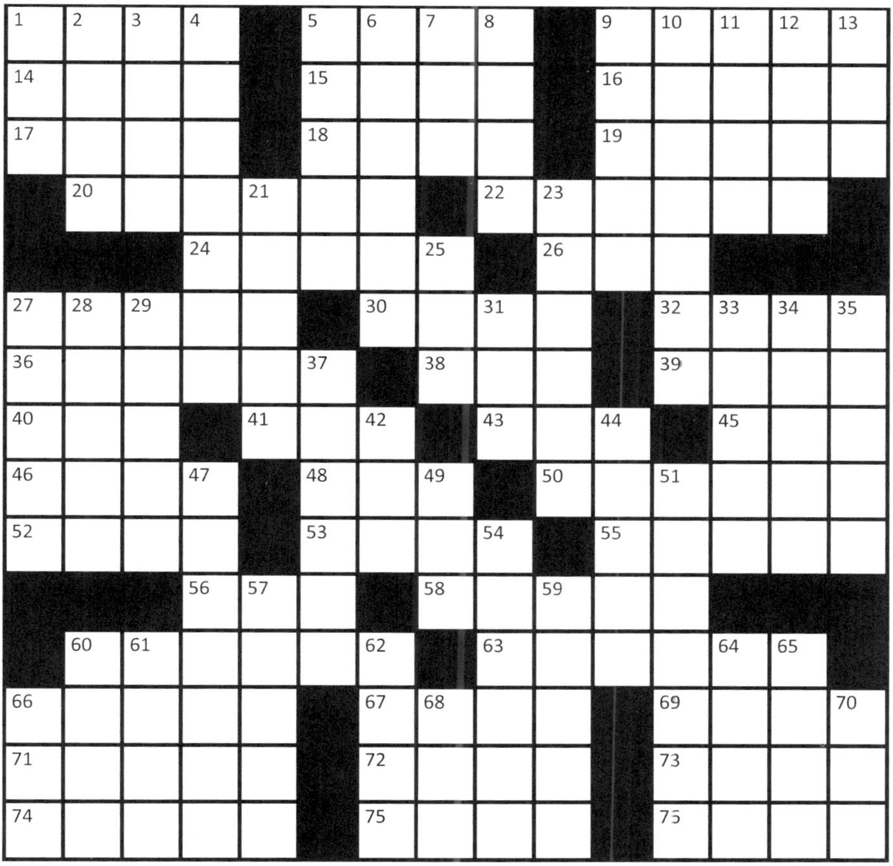

29. Capitol Filmworks camera brand
31. AAA handout
33. *I Had a Hammer* author
34. Cold Stone Creamery utensil
35. Easy mark
37. Resembling rural Alabama
42. "___ whiz!"
44. Symbol of thinness
47. Soaking mistake? (2 wds.)
49. Scottish cap
51. Billionaire construction titan from Mountain Brook and anagram of 4-, 10- and 47-Down
54. Make queasy
57. Broadcast on WBMA-TV
59. Final authority
60. Carve in stone
61. Surin West cuisine
62. Scarf material, often
64. Hodgepodge
65. Defense alliance acronym
66. Lanett's winter hrs.
68. *Dothan Eagle* society page word
70. Auburn volleyball court divider

Musicians

There is no better example of the Alabama music scene than the band Alabama.

Formed in Fort Payne in 1969 by Randy Owen and his cousin Teddy Gentry, the country music/southern rock/gospel/pop band continues to perform and record. They have had 30 No. 1 hits and sold more than 70 million records.

Jimmy Buffett, of Fairhope, created his own genre of music coupled with a lifestyle and an entourage of fans known as Parrotheads. His biggest hits include "Margaritaville," "Come Monday" and "Cheeseburger in Paradise."

Nat King Cole (Montgomery) was a jazz pianist whose silky voice made him a star for decades. He recorded more than 100 albums. His first No. 1 hit was "(I Love You) For Sentimental Reasons"; his most memorable hits include "Mona Lisa" and "Unforgettable."

Bobby Goldsboro (Dothan) left Auburn University after his sophomore year to pursue a music career. He wound up with three No. 1 hits ("Honey," "Watching Scotty Grow" and "Muddy Mississippi Line") and a popular TV variety show.

Lionel Richie (Tuskegee) achieved fame as a member of the Commodores, but achieved superstar status as a solo performer, recording a dozen No. 1 hits beginning with "Endless Love" in 1981 and ending with "Do It to Me" in 1992.

Toni Tennille (Montgomery) was half of the Grammy Award-winning duo Captain & Tennille. She also performed with Pink Floyd, Art Garfunkel, Elton John and The Beach Boys.

Mervyn Warren (Huntsville) has won five Grammy Awards as a composer and gospel performer. He has done the score for dozens of movies and TV shows, including Disney's *Sister Act 2*.

Although Chubby Checker most often gets credit for singing and inventing "The Twist," it was Hank Ballard (Bessemer) who wrote and originally recorded the song.

Lionel Hampton (Birmingham) ranks among the all-time greats in jazz. His awards include a National Medal of Arts, National Endowment for the Arts Fellowship, Hollywood Walk of Fame, Papal Medal and induction into the Alabama Jazz Hall of Fame.

Alabama musicians are well represented in every part of a music store:

- Jazz—Chalmers Alford (Huntsville), Cleve Eaton (Birmingham), Urbie Green (Mobile), Erskine Hawkins (Birmingham), Grover Mitchell (Whatley), Sun Ra (Birmingham), Ray Reach (Birmingham), Johnny Smith (Birmingham), Ward Swingle (Mobile), Ken Watters (Huntsville) and Cootie Williams (Mobile).
- Soul—Clarence Carter (Montgomery), various members of The Temptations (Dennis Edwards, Melvin Franklin, Eddie Kendricks and Paul Williams), Wilson Pickett (Prattville) and Percy Sledge (Leighton).
- Country—William Lee Golden (East Brewton), Vern Gosdin (Woodland), Emmylou Harris (Birmingham), Sonny James (Hackleburg), Jamey Johnson (Montgomery), Shelby Lynne (Frankville), Ashton Shepherd (Coffeeville), Neil Thrasher (Birmingham), Hank Williams (Georgiana), Hank Williams Jr. (Cullman) and Tammy Wynette (Red Bay).
- Rap—Rich Boy (Mobile), Gucci Mane (Birmingham), Matchstik (Dothan) and Yelawolf (Gadsden).
- Broadway Show Tunes—Nell Carter (Birmingham) and Rebecca Luker (Helena).
- Blues—W.C. Handy (Florence), Jimmy Lee Sudduth (Fayette) and Dinah Washington (Tuscaloosa).
- *American Idol* Alumni—Bo Bice (Helena), Diana DeGarmo (Birmingham), Taylor Hicks (Hoover) and Ruben Studdard (Birmingham).

Musicians Crossword

Solution on page 148.

Across

1. 2006 *American Idol* winner who grew up in Hoover
6. Fort Payne native who was one of the founding members of the group Alabama
10. Bo, from Huntsville, who knows his music
14. Not burning yet
15. Voting no at a Decatur City Council meeting
16. Riding the waves of the Gulf
17. Off one's rocker
18. Sunset Landing Golf Club shot
19. Bed board at Ashley Furniture
20. Poker pot starter
21. Mexican moolah
22. Stage
23. Ivan the Terrible, e.g.
25. Introductory reading for a UA class
26. Funny business
29. Eagle's claw
31. Author Jong
32. Lionel Richie's glow
33. Alabama State Fair animal with horns
37. *Alabaster News* obituary datum
38. "Cheeseburger in Paradise" singer who calls Fairhope his hometown
41. Solemn promise
42. Numskull
44. Pro ___
45. Muscat native
47. Goes like the dickens on I-65
49. Cracker Barrel breakfast order
50. Subdued color
53. Copycat
54. Redstone Arsenal tanks and such
55. Desire
57. Toothed item at Norm's Barber Shop
61. Quick cut at Big League Barbers
62. Birmingham Yellow Cab vehicle
63. Part of a WCOV-TV feed
64. Auburn fraternity letter
65. Decorates a cake at Mary's Cakes & Pastries
66. More twisted, as humor
67. Lead singer of Alabama who hails from Fort Payne
68. Montgomery-born baritone, Nat King ___
69. 1999 Grammy winner for Best New Artist who lived in Mobile

Down

1. 2006 Hawaii bowl game featuring Bama's Anthony Madison
2. Aware of (2 wds.)
3. Congeal, as blood
4. Energizing
5. Alabama hog farm pen
6. Escapade
7. Heavy load
8. "Beetle Bailey" pooch
9. Hobby Lobby buy
10. Hitting hard
11. Religion of the Koran
12. Discontinue
13. Shula's Steak House diner
21. Salary from Birmingham Steel Corp.
22. Prattville Country Club instructor
24. Poke holes in
25. Point to Point Land Surveyors map
26. Its symbol is Pb in a Foley HS science class
27. Start of a conclusion
28. Competed
29. Campus in Medford, Mass.
30. Carpetland USA calculation
32. A long way off, like California

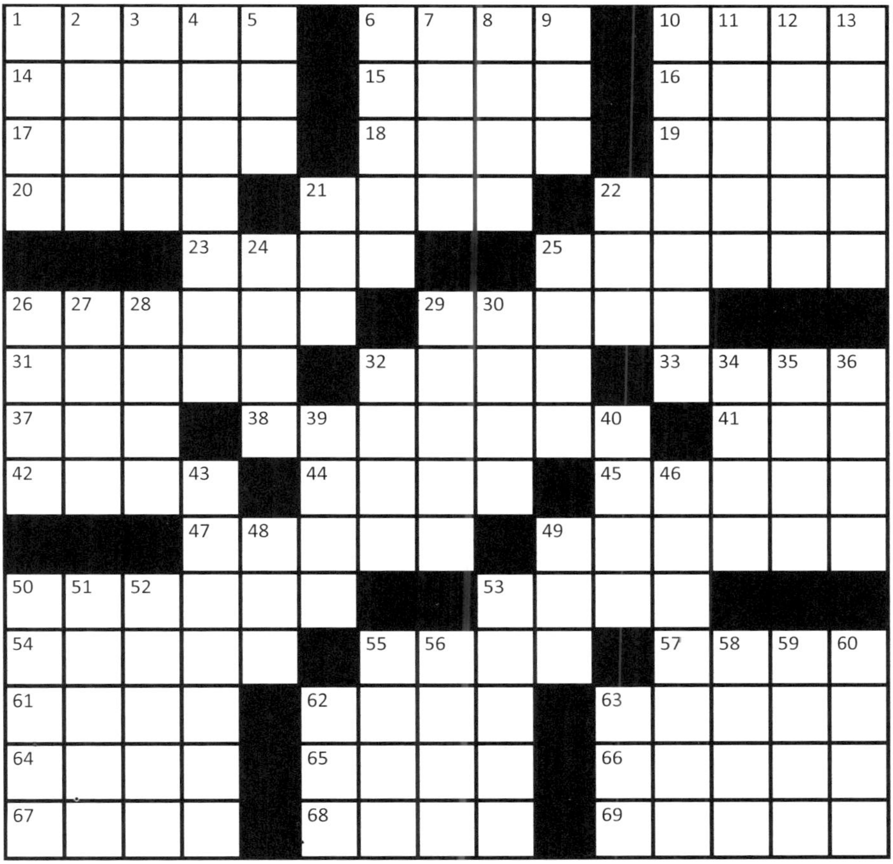

34. East Alabama Motor Speedway track shape
35. LongHorn Steakhouse sauce
36. Twerp
39. Russian mountain range
40. Hefty volume from the UAB library
43. Furniture Warehouse hassock
46. Our solar system's smallest planet
48. Always, in verse
49. Select, with "for"
50. Place for a barbecue, maybe
51. You might wait for it at a US 43 stoplight
52. Whack, biblically
53. Licoricelike flavor
55. Baylor's home
56. Figure skating jump
58. Chief Norse god
59. Bearing
60. Yawner at The Comedy Club
62. ___-tac-toe
63. Hall & Smith Shoe Repair Shop tool

Star Crossed

Place the letters at the bottom of each grid into the empty squares to form the first and last names of six musicians with Alabama connections. Solutions of page 148.

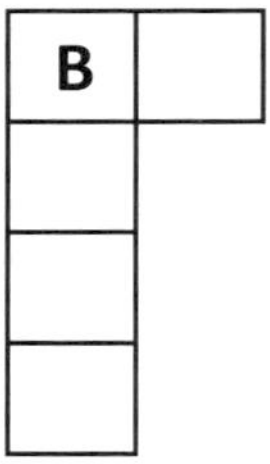

1. C E I O

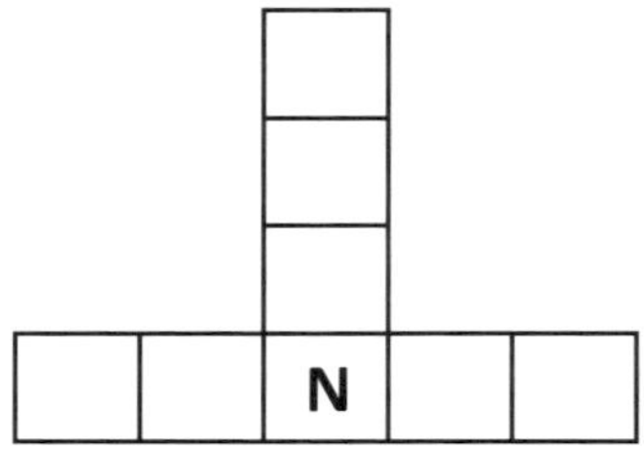

2. A D E O R W Y

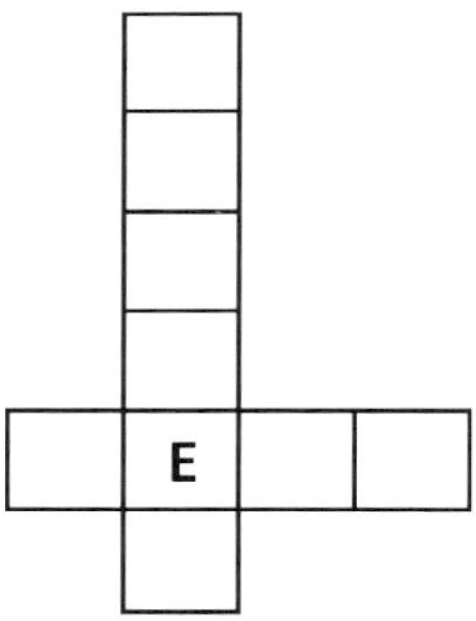

3. A C L L N R R T

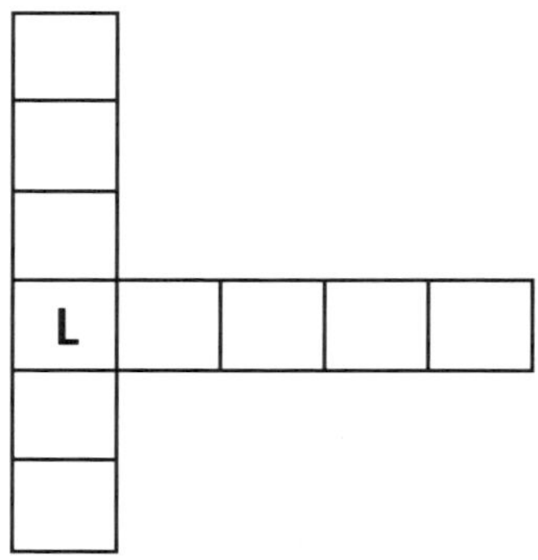

4. B E E H N N S Y Y

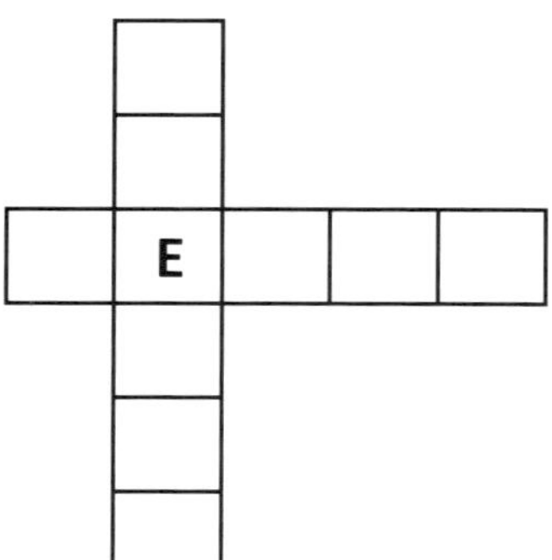

5. C D E G L P R S Y

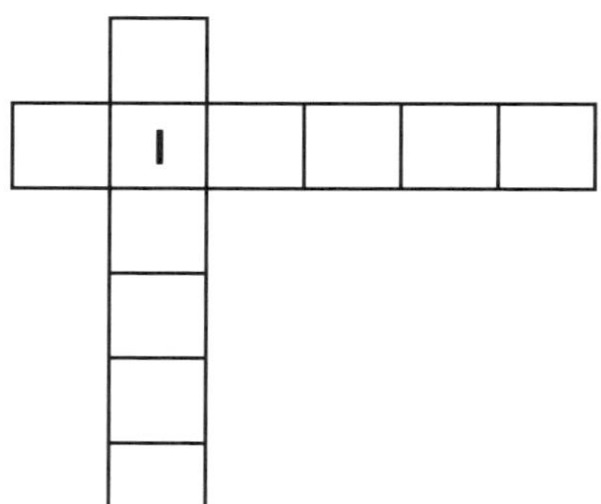

6. C E E H I L L N O R

SHAW WASH

Tommy Shaw was born and raised in Montgomery. The guitarist-songwriter joined the rock band Styx in 1975 and helped the group reach international fame. Shaw was inducted into the Alabama Music Hall of Fame in 2009. The letters S-H-A-W can be arranged to form 24 different combinations. Here are 21 of those combinations. Which three are missing? Solution on page 148.

SAWH	HSWA	AWSH	WSHA	WASH	HWAS	SWAH
AHSW	WSAH	HAWS	AHWS	AWHS	WHSA	HSAW
WHAS	SHAW	SHWA	HASW	SAHW	ASHW	WAHS

Alford Sudoku

Use logic to fill in the grid so every row, column and 2x3 box contains the letters A-L-F-O-R-D, in honor of Chalmers Alford. The three-time Grammy Award winning jazz guitarist died in Huntsville in 2008 at the age of 52. Solution on page 148.

R		A	O		F
					A
		F	A		
		L	F		
A					
F		D	L		R

Politicians

Alabama has not had a U.S. President with direct ties to the state. Alabama does boast one U.S. Vice President: William R. King.

King was born in North Carolina, but moved to King's Bend (between present-day Selma and Cahaba) in Dallas County when he returned to the U.S. after serving as a delegate overseas. At the age of 33, he was elected U.S. Senator from Alabama and served for 29 years. King was elected Vice President in 1852 (on the Democratic ticket with Franklin Pierce) and was sworn in on Mar. 24, 1953, in Cuba. He was in Cuba, hoping to recover from tuberculosis. (King is the only U.S. President or Vice President to take the oath of office on foreign soil.) He died three weeks later without performing any official duties of the office. He is buried in Selma's Live Oak Cemetery.

The first governor of Alabama was William Wyatt Bibb (1817-19 for the Alabama Territory and 1819-20 after Alabama became a state). After dying in office, Bibb was succeeded by his brother, Thomas Bibb.

Officially, there have been 53 governors. The longest serving (and maybe the most controversial) was George C. Wallace, who served 16 years over four non-consecutive terms. Only one woman has served as governor: George Wallace's wife, Lurleen.

George C. Wallace was born in Clio and elected governor in 1962 after using racist messages in the campaign. "You know, I tried to talk about good roads and good schools and all these things that have been part of my career, and nobody listened," he said. "And then I began talking about n------, and they stomped the floor."

Wallace attempted to preserve segregation. He tried to block African-American students from entering the University of Alabama and elementary schools in Huntsville. He said: "The President (John F. Kennedy) wants us to surrender this state to Martin Luther King and his group of pro-communists who have instituted these demonstrations."

Wallace was dubbed "the most influential loser" in 20th century politics after four unsuccessful runs for the U.S. Presidency. He was paralyzed after being shot in 1972 and used a wheelchair for the remainder of his life.

The current governor is Robert J. Bentley, a Republican who took office on Jan. 17, 2011.

The current U.S. Senators for Alabama are Richard Shelby, a Birmingham native who has served since 1987, and Jeff Sessions III, a Selma native who was first elected in 1996.

The longest serving Alabama U.S. Senators were John Sparkman (1946-79) and J. Lister Hill (1938-69).

The Alabama State Capitol was designated a National Historic Landmark in 1962.

U.S. Supreme Court Justices from Alabama were John McKinley (1837-52), John Archibald Campbell (1853-61), William Burnham Woods (1881-87) and Hugo Black (1937-71).

Black was born in Ashland in Clay County and enrolled at Birmingham Medical School when he was 17 years old. He quickly dropped out of med school and enrolled at the University of Alabama School of Law. Black practiced law until he joined the U.S. Army in World War I. When he returned from the military, Black ran for the U.S. Senate and joined the Ku Klux Klan, thinking it necessary for his political career. He later said that his membership in the KKK was a mistake, but it helped get him elected to the Senate. He served in the U.S. Senate for 10+ years before being nominated by President Franklin D. Roosevelt to join the Supreme Court.

Other Alabamans who had high-ranking positions in the U.S. government include Condoleezza Rice (Birmingham), the Secretary of State under George W. Bush; Alexis Herman (Mobile), the Secretary of Labor under Bill Clinton; and Winton Blount (Union Springs), the U.S. Postmaster General under Richard Nixon.

Politicians Crossword

Solution on page 149.

Across

1. Ready and willing's partner
5. Al's Flowers bud holder
9. Sculptures on pedestals at the Birmingham Museum of Art
14. Alabama Gulf Coast Zoo big cat
15. Litmus reddener in a Holtville HS science class
16. 180 on US 80, so to speak
17. Alabama Symphony Orchestra reed instrument
18. Huntsville Dermatology Associates concern
19. Montgomery County Historical Society photo color
20. Talladega National Forest tree
21. Eclipse phenomenon
23. WWII British fliers
24. Man in the photo
26. Citizen Kane's estate
29. Part of TGIF
30. PNC Bank offering, for short
31. "Ta-ta!"
34. Phonograph needle at Eastbrook Antique Mall
38. Decompose
39. Mobile BayBears pitcher's stat
40. WKRG-TV news reader
44. PG or R at CineStar of Huntsville
47. "Without any further ___ . . ."
48. Tuskegee University psych class topic
49. Queasy feeling
52. Workplace for the man in the photo
57. Under the weather
58. Resembling some lines
60. Alabama State Capitol VIP
61. ___-gritty
64. Zap with a Homewood Police Department Taser
65. 1492 ship of note
66. Like Maple Hill Cemetery at night
67. Give temporarily
68. Ran, as colors
69. Kroger ginger cookies
70. Table scraps
71. Relinquish

Down

1. CVS hand lotion additive
2. Hill Crest Baptist Church holy book
3. Pioneer Museum of Alabama weaving machines
4. Mobile-to-Dothan dir.
5. Scram
6. Kind of squash at the Enterprise Farmers Market
7. Alabama farm towers
8. St. Clair County town named after a Genesis location
9. Jefferson County Transit Authority transport
10. American Indian Museum tribe
11. Old model at Bill Penney Toyota
12. Threesome
13. Mix-up
21. It follows Pell and Rainbow in Alabama
22. Line on a graph in an Etowah HS math class
25. Bro or sis
27. Matt Jones Gallery item
28. Florence City Council no vote
31. Victoria's Secret purchase
32. "Silent Night" adjective

33. Mail Boxes ___
35. Kempani Hawaiian Grill garland
36. Hughes Crematory ashes holder
37. Droop
41. Suffers from
42. "___ to Billie Joe"
43. Alabama highway
44. Transmits twice
45. Like fine wine at Filet & Vine
46. Montgomery Air Freight weight
49. Dressed to the ___
50. UFO pilot
51. The U of UHF
52. Out-and-out
53. Movie double's task
54. Nimble as a UA gymnast
55. Fit as a UA gymnast
56. Sidestep
59. Nobel Peace Prize city
62. 15% to 20%, for a Ruth's Chris waiter
63. "Absolutely!"
65. WSFA-TV's network affiliation

ALABAMA GOVERNORS WORD SEARCH

Solution on page 149.

N E S C O L E W I S Y J M C L
U E H N O T T A P W A T T S R
T E Y U S B I L C J E D M H S
N R E W E R B L N J S I I M Y
U O L I N D S A Y O T X B I Z
H O S R O L M C S H D O M L O
L M A R J L L E Y N H N L L K
G Y E H E N D E R S O N A E I
P E B G A T L E W T N S D R L
M L E U G T T T U O W E R X B
O I P G N R J A T N D H O E Y
S R K E O E A S P B Y C F W P
L P B H L M U V K J J A M E S
O T S K W O A T E S K R A P S
F O S K H C P A R S O N S A M

BEASLEY	ENDERSON	LINDSAY	RILEY
BENTLEY	HOUSTON	MCDOWELL	SAMFORD
BRANDON	HUNT	MILLER	SEAY
BREWER	JAMES	MOORE	SHORTER
COBB	JELKS	OATES	SIEGELMAN
COMER	JOHNSTON	PARSONS	SMITH
DIXON	JONES	PATTERSON	SPARKS
FOLSOM	KILBY	PATTON	WALLACE
GRAVES	LEWIS	PERSONS	WATTS

BUILD THE NAMES

Use the letter groups—one at the beginning and one at the end—to build the last names of U.S. Senators from Alabama. Each letter group will be used once. Solution on page 149.

AN ART BAN BY DE EAD HE IN

MAN MO ON ONS SES SH SPA ST

1. ___ SI ___
2. ___ KH ___
3. ___ RK ___
4. ___ NT ___
5. ___ FL ___
6. ___ RG ___
7. ___ EW ___
8. ___ EL ___

WOMEN

Rosa Parks wasn't the first African-American who refused to give up her seat on a bus to a white passenger, but she was the first who challenged the order in court. And with that challenge on Dec. 1, 1955, in Montgomery, she became an icon of resistance to racial segregation.

Parks was born in Tuskegee, moved to Montgomery and got married. She had various jobs and served as secretary of the local chapter of the NAACP. She rode the bus to and from her work as a seamstress. About the specific event, she later recalled: "When that white driver stepped back toward us, when he waved his hand and ordered us up and out of our seats, I felt a determination cover my body like a quilt on a winter night."

Parks was arrested, found guilty of violating a local ordinance and fined $10, plus $4 in court costs. Less than a year later, the U.S. Supreme Court ruled that segregation on public transportation was illegal and African-American passengers were able to sit anywhere they wanted.

The lone female governor in Alabama was Lurleen Wallace. She served from Jan. 16, 1967, until her death on May 7, 1968. She grew up in Tuscaloosa and was working at Kresge's Five and Dime when she met her future husband, George C. Wallace. She succeeded her husband as governor.

Mia Hamm (Selma) was called by *The Washington Post* columnist Michael Wilbon, "the most important athlete of the last 15 years." She is perhaps the greatest female soccer player in history, scoring more goals (158) in international competition than any player, male or female. She was elected to the National Soccer Hall of Fame and her silhouette is on the Women's Professional Soccer logo.

The Alabama Women's Hall of Fame was established in 1970 and inducted its first class the following year. The initial inductees were Helen Keller, Hallie Farmer and Julia Strudwick

Tutwiler. (The museum is located on the campus of Judson College in Marion.)

Keller was born in Tuscumbia in 1880. She became blind and deaf when she contracted an illness at the age of 19 months. Keller's struggles to overcome her disabilities are chronicled in numerous books. She wrote 12 books herself. Keller received the Presidential Medal of Freedom from Lyndon B. Johnson, was elected to the National Women's Hall of Fame and her image is on the back of the Alabama state quarter.

Farmer was a political scientist, educator, author and prison reformer. While teaching at Alabama College (now the University of Montevallo), she was active in a number of women's organizations and was described by the Birmingham News as "the undisputed champion of Alabama's politically-minded women."

Tutwiler, a native of Tuscaloosa, was an advocate for education and prison reform and served as president of Livingston Normal College (now the University of West Alabama). She was called "the mother of co-education in Alabama" and "the angel of the prisons."

Other inductees through the years have included Dixie Bibb Graves (the first Alabama woman elected to the U.S. Senate), Tallulah Bankhead (actress, talk-show host and *bonne vivante*), Chrysostom Moynahan (the first Registered Nurse licensed in Alabama), Geneva Mercer (sculptor whose work includes the Flimp Fountain at the Montgomery Museum of Fine Arts), Zelda Sayre Fitzgerald (author, ballerina, painter and wife of F. Scott Fitzgerald), Hattie Hooker Wilkins (promoter of woman's suffrage and the first woman elected to the Alabama Legislature), Juliet Opie Hopkins (Civil War nurse who was known as "Florence Nightingale of the South") and Coretta Scott King (author, civil rights activist and wife of Martin Luther King Jr.).

Women Crossword

Solution on page 149.

Across

1. Hefty competitor at Winn-Dixie
5. "___ I care!" (2 wds.)
9. Open-mouthed
14. Former U.S. Secretary of State who is from Birmingham
15. Old Daniel Pratt Cotton ___ Dam
16. U.S. Senator from Alabama who succeeded her husband in 1978
17. Riverside Casino buy-in
18. Talladega Speedway wheel shaft
19. More than unpopular
20. Dictator
22. Bankhead National Forest tree juice
24. End of many company names in Alabama
25. Rod at a pig roast
27. "___ alive!"
29. John, Paul and John Paul
32. Like Siberian winters
35. Trendy, as a downtown Birmingham bar
38. Lincoln HS geometry calculation
39. PC key
40. Singer Yoko
41. Kia of Gadsden auto name
42. First black woman to travel in space who is a native of Decatur
43. Alabama cornfield sound
44. Former UA quarterback Stabler
45. Odd
46. Resembling most Miss Alabama contestants
47. Devious and cunning
48. Runway walker
49. Pessimists at Wells Fargo Advisors
50. Decide to leave, with "out"
51. Old Italian bread?
53. Use an alley at Leland Lanes
56. Bessemer BPOE member
59. Put a ship to shore in the Gulf
63. Wear away a Choctawhatchee River bank
65. Not taken in by
67. Vestavia Hills HS debate side
68. Member of the Communist Party and Black Panther Party who was born in Birmingham
69. Shannon Mine find
70. MLK's wife who was a native of Heiberger
71. Catch forty winks at Red Roof Inn
72. Sacred bird of ancient Egypt
73. MOB flight data, briefly

Down

1. ASU alum
2. Pickup shtick in a Tuscaloosa bar?
3. Performs for the Montevallo Main Street Players
4. Type of diving in the Gulf
5. Valuable violin
6. Number of points for a Crimson Tide touchdown
7. Misfortunes
8. Kind of collar from Countryside Veterinary Hospital
9. Sound at Spa Elia
10. Tumbler at Cricket's Restaurant
11. Fultondale HS choir voice
12. Hammer's end
13. Some Waterloo HS linemen
21. Governor Bentley photo ___ (media events)
23. Anniston native Michael Curry, as a Detroit cager
26. Like some amusement parks
28. Alabama hit: "___ Again"
29. Tuskegee native who refused to give up her seat on a bus
30. Bay window in an Elite Builders home
31. Spring bloom

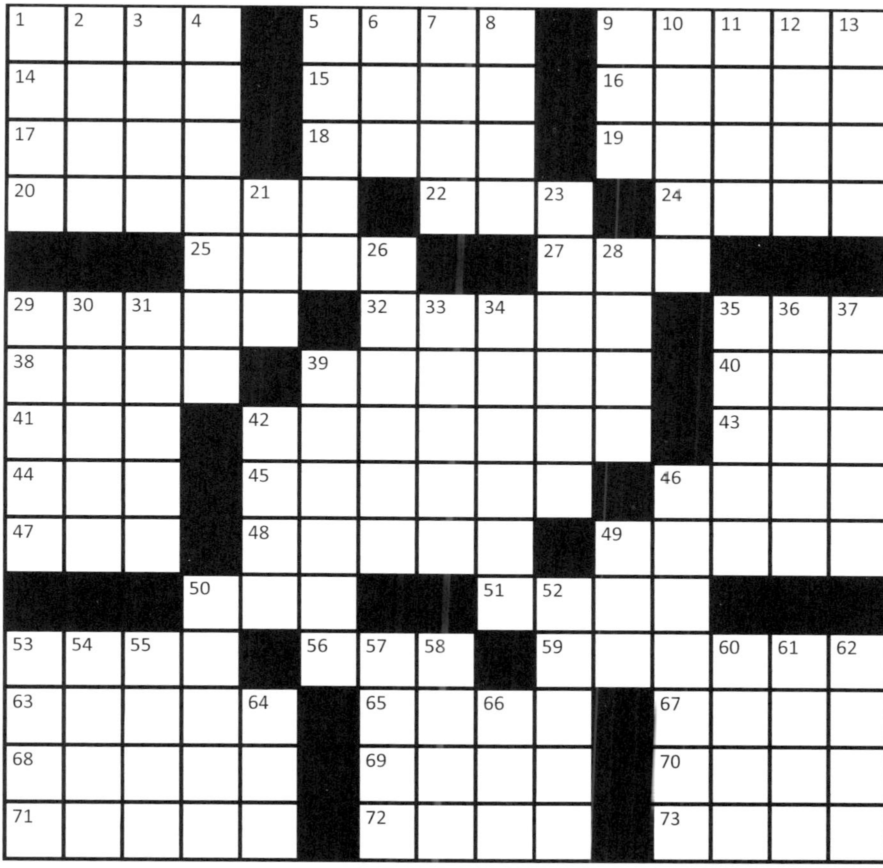

33. Breathing
34. Scalp a Saenger Theatre concert ticket
35. O Kafes Coffee shop order
36. WCRL studio sign (2 wds.)
37. 2005 Miss America from Pelham
39. Indicate
42. Start, as a dead battery
46. Scone relative
49. Sis' sib
50. WGAD song from the '80s
52. Bice, DeGarmo, Hicks and Studdard
53. Jackson Hospital units
54. Type of surgery at the UA School of Dentistry
55. Made a rug
57. Centers of activity
58. Door feature
60. Make a sweater
61. Sicilian erupter
62. Excavates at the Liddell Archeological Site
64. Clairvoyant's gift
66. Mac's Tavern drink: Mai ___

CRYPTIC QUOTE

The Cryptic Quote is a substitution cipher in which one letter stands for another. If you think that A equals Z, it will equal Z throughout the puzzle. Solve this Cryptic Quote from Mobile native Dr. Regina Benjamin, who was named the U.S. Surgeon General in 2009. (HINT: Every Q here is actually an O.) Solution on page 149.

" J   U G I   W Z   G

N Q J U Z   J I   B E Z

F Q N Z F Z I B   B Q

J F A O Q N Z   Q D O

I G B J Q I ' R   E Z G Y B E

U G O Z   G I V   Q D O

I G B J Q I ' R   E Z G Y B E .

J   X G I B   B Q   W Z

R D O Z   B E G B   I Q

Q I Z   T G Y Y R

B E O Q D L E   B E Z

U O G U S R   G R   X Z

J F A O Q N Z   Q D O

E Z G Y B E   U G O Z

R M R B Z F . "

WALKER SUDOKU

Use logic to fill in the grid so every row, column and 2x3 box contains the letters W-A-L-K-E-R, in honor of Margaret Walker. The Birmingham native was a well-known African-American poet and writer. Solution on page 150.

		L			
	A	R	W		
		A	E	K	
	K	W	R		
		E	A	R	
			L		

WHO AM I? SUDOKU

Use logic to fill in the boxes so every row, column and 3x3 box contains the letters to the last name of the Montgomery native who was the first black female attorney in Alabama, admitted to the bar in 1948. When completed, her name will be spelled correctly in the row indicated by the arrow. Solution on page 149.

			O		S	I	E		
	I	C				D			
	R			E			C		
			N	S				R	E
►									
	E	R				O	I		
			K			S			D
				O				K	S
			R	I	K		O		

OTHERS

Among the earliest people of note where present-day Alabama exists is a quartet of Native American chiefs: Tuskaloosa, a paramount chief in a tribe that was an ancestor to the Choctaw and Creek in the 16th century; Alexander McGillivray (a.k.a. Hoboi-Hili-Miko), a principal chief of the Creek from 1782-93; William Weatherford (a.k.a. Red Eagle), a Creek chief during the Creek War (1813-14); and Billy Powell (a.k.a. Osceola), an influential Seminole leader in the early 19th century.

Booker T. Washington became the first leader of Tuskegee Normal and Industrial Institute and headed it from 1881 until his death in 1915. He was the dominant African-American leader in the U.S. for 25 years, speaking on behalf of Southern blacks who had lost their right to vote.

Washington was born into slavery, but after the Civil War, he walked 500 miles to attend the Hampton Normal Agricultural Institute in Virginia. After graduating, he began teaching and eventually was recommended for the job of heading the Tuskegee Institute. He pushed education and job training as the path to self-reliance and success. He was often criticized by other African-Americans for suggesting blacks accept an inferior status as they worked to improve themselves in the future. He was asked for advice on race relations by Presidents Theodore Roosevelt and William Howard Taft. Washington founded the National Negro Business League in 1900 and wrote an autobiography (*Up From Slavery)* in 1901.

Other Alabamans who have left their mark include: Pat Garrett of Chambers County (who was the New Mexico lawman who killed Billy the Kid in 1881); Gen. Holland "Howlin' Mad" Smith of Russell County (who is called "the father of modern U.S. amphibious warfare"); Edward A. Burkhalter of Roanoke (who was a Vice Admiral in the U.S. Navy, the Chief of Naval Intelligence and the Defense Intelligence Agency's Chief of Staff); and astronauts N.

Jan Davis of Huntsville (a veteran of three missions, logging 673 hours in space), Joe F. Edwards Jr. of Lineville (who traveled 3.6 million miles while orbiting Earth 138 times as part of a Space Shuttle-Mir docking mission) and Mae C. Jemison of Decatur (the first African-American woman to travel in space while aboard the Space Shuttle *Endeavour* in 1992).

Also: Fred Thompson of Sheffield (who served as a U.S. Senator from Tennessee for eight years, ran for President and spent time as a Hollywood actor); Robert Gibbs of Auburn (who was President Barack Obama's first Press Secretary); Angela Davis of Birmingham (who was active in the Communist Party USA and Black Panther Party in the 1960s and '70s); Heather Whitestone of Dothan (who was the 1995 Miss America despite being deaf); and Chris Dickerson of Montgomery (a bodybuilder who held the title of Mr. Olympia at the age of 43).

And: Betty Lou Gerson of Birmingham (the voice actress who made Cruella de Vil of *One Hundred and One Dalmatians* scary to millions of youngsters); Howard Hill of Wilsonville (a football and basketball player at Auburn University who earned the title of World's Greatest Archer that led to him appearing in nine films); Bill Holbrook of Huntsville (a comic strip artist who draws and writes *On the Fastrack*); and Alan Hunter of Birmingham (one of the original five MTV VeeJays).

And finally, there's James "Sawyer" Ford. The fictional character from the TV show *Lost* was played by Josh Holloway. Sawyer was "born" in Jasper. He was on the tragic Flight 815 from Australia after being deported for assaulting an Aussie politician. Sawyer was portrayed as a conniving, sarcastic handsome flirt who collected items that washed ashore. In the series finale, he escaped the island on an airplane with five others.

Others Crossword

Solution on page 150.

Across

1. Leak slowly
5. Alabama state tree offering
10. Put one's foot down
14. Cathedral or Rickwood, e.g.
15. Like one who errs, so they say
16. Medical breakthrough
17. Blue Moon Cyber Cafe patron
18. Tiny organism: Var.
19. RSA Battle House Tower elevator name
20. U.S. Surgeon General who hails from Mobile
22. Native of Union Springs who was the U.S. Postmaster General
24. Good way to rest
25. Soma Intimates lingerie item
26. University of South Alabama color
27. Hibbett Sports shareholder's goal
28. Birmingham Barons bat wood
31. Angel's Deli carrier
34. Three sheets to the wind
35. Oak Ridge Boys star: William ___ Golden
36. Donny Osmond song: "Run To ___"
37. Cut rinds, e.g.
39. ALDOT road crew supply
40. 1996 Olympic torch lighter
41. Gibbs Farm wooly animal
42. Oak Hill Cemetery resting place
43. Tie the knot at Sweet Gum Bottom Chapel
44. Cable TV sports award
45. Autauga County School District org.
47. Alabama Symphony Orchestra instrument held with two hands
48. Blunder (2 wds.)
52. Educator in agriculture at Tuskegee Institute for 47 years
55. German rocket scientist who worked in Huntsville for 20+ years
56. Length x width, for a rectangle
57. Blazing
59. Taj Mahal city
60. Fish story teller at Lake Pickwick
61. Kind of CVS spray
62. Go like heck on I-20
63. Birmingham's Our ___ of Lourdes Catholic Church
64. Death row reprieves from Governor Bentley
65. Scottish Gaelic

Down

1. Southern Skin Divers Supply tank
2. Lets up
3. Makes level
4. Swearing falsely in a Baldwin County Court
5. In disgrace
6. Like Alabama in July
7. Brookwood Baptist Church prayer ending
8. Tiny bit
9. Providing legal power
10. Brusters Ice Cream utensil
11. Alabama Ballet attire
12. Redbox rental: ___ *Brockovich*
13. Orkin's target
21. "___ we there yet?"
23. Pines Golf Course, e.g.

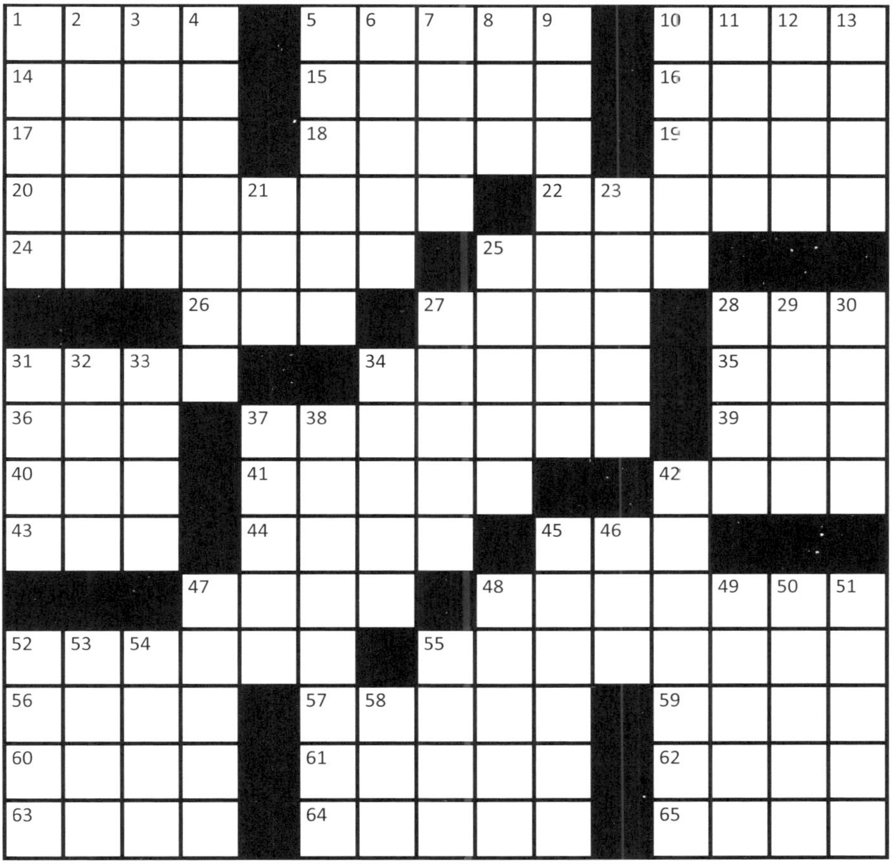

25. Johnson Pools & Spas choice
27. Resembling a dirty kitchen
28. Beauregard HS choir voice
29. Young Tailor clothes line
30. Parsley or sage
31. Microwave option
32. Anger, with "up"
33. In the center of
34. Hang loosely
37. Lyman Ward Military Academy freshman
38. Losers in an Alabama election
42. Percentage listed in an IRS booklet (2 wds.)
45. Discussion groups
46. Margarine container
47. Alabama Fertility Specialists egg producer
48. Raid
49. Beeper for an Elmore Community Hospital doctor
50. Saintly glows
51. Alabama Department of Conservation and Natural Resources trap
52. Ring up
53. Mobile Opera highlight
54. Peruse the *Selma Times-Journal*
55. AMEX alternative at Target
58. Jenny Craig dieter's concern

She Said What?

Fill in the blanks with the words below to complete a quote from Huntsville native Paula Poundstone, a stand-up comic. Solution on page 150.

" I WAS __________ IN __________, BUT I __________

__________ THERE __________ A __________

__________ I'D __________ __________ __________

WAS TO __________ . "

ALABAMA	DONE	MONTH
BEFORE	EVERYTHING	ONLY
BORN	FOR	THERE
DO	LIVED	

TXT NAMES

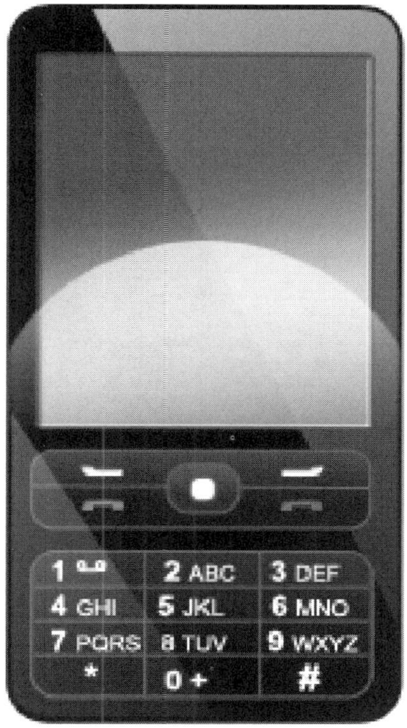

Use your cell phone keypad to help decode the last names of these famous people from Alabama. In the example 72757, the 7 could be P, Q, R or S; the 2 could be A, B or C; the next 7 could be P, Q, R or S; the 5 could be J, K or L; and the last 7 could be P, Q, R or S. The person's name found in that text is PARKS, civil rights activist Rosa Parks. Now try these. Solutions on page 150.

1. 7423 (Former U.S. Secretary of State born in Birmingham.)
2. 44227 (Auburn native who was President Obama's first press secretary.)
3. 36967 (2005 Miss America from Birmingham.)
4. 53279 (Psychedelic drug advocate who graduated from UA.)
5. 92537 (Co-founder of Wikipedia.)
6. 25536 (Long-time Yankees announcer from Birmingham.)
7. 569637 (Tuskegee native with a nationally syndicated radio show.)
8. 5364766 (Decatur native who was the first African-American woman to travel in space.)

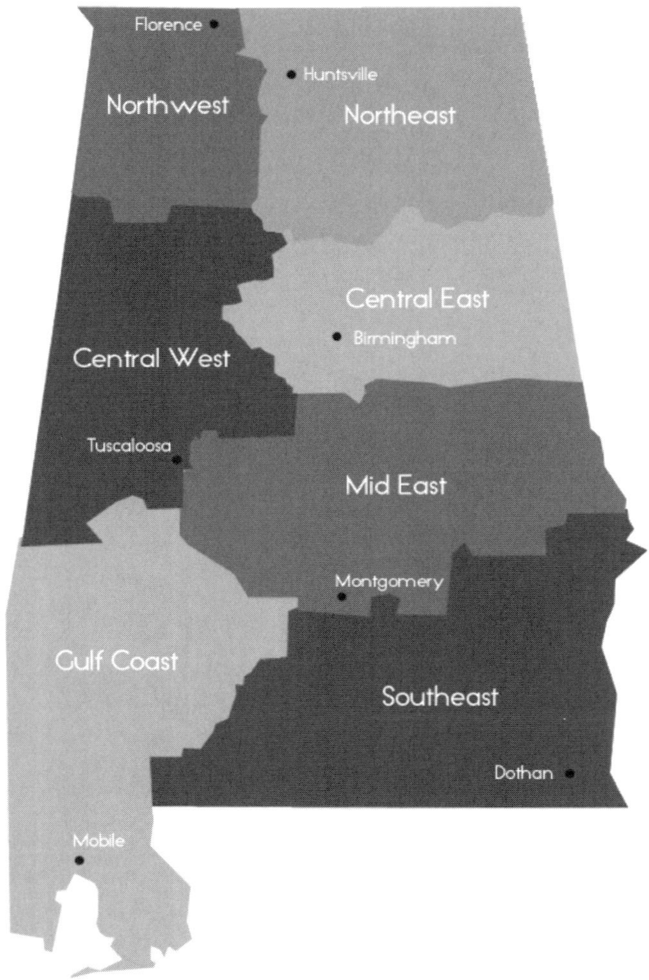
Florence
Huntsville
Northwest
Northeast
Central East
Birmingham
Central West
Tuscaloosa
Mid East
Montgomery
Gulf Coast
Southeast
Dothan
Mobile

Part II: Alabama Regions

NORTHWEST

The Northwest region of Alabama is bisected by the Tennessee River. The resulting Wilson Lake and Wheeler Lake give the area plenty of water activities.

The region is also home to "The Shoals" metropolitan area, made up of the Quad Cities: Florence, Muscle Shoals, Tuscumbia and Sheffield.

Florence is the largest city in the area. The county seat of Lauderdale County, Florence has a population of 40,000. It is a host to the W.C. Handy Music Festival and the Renaissance Faire. Florence is home to the University of North Alabama and the site of the only Frank Lloyd Wright-designed home (Rosenbaum House) in the state.

Muscle Shoals (population 13,000) is home to FAME Studios (and the Muscle Shoals Sound Studio is just down the road). Among the stars that have recorded and developed their work in the region are Aretha Franklin, the Rolling Stones, Rod Stewart, Eric Clapton, Lynyrd Skynyrd, The Allman Brothers, George Michael and Carrie Underwood. Stars with homes in the area include George Strait, Tim McGraw and Faith Hill.

Natural bridges, like the one shown above, are very common around the state of Alabama.

Tuscumbia (population 8,500) was the hometown of Helen Keller and is the site of the Alabama Music Hall of Fame. Named after Chief Tuscomby in the early 19th century, it is the county seat of Colbert County.

The Miracle Worker, featuring the original water pump near where Helen discovered language, is staged every summer at the Keller homesite.

Sheffield (population 9,000) is the hometown of former U.S. Senator Fred Thompson, Watergate committee member Sen. Howell Heflin, country-soul pioneer Arthur Alexander and French horn player Willie Ruff.

Winfield (population 4,500) is home to the annual Mule Day. The festival was chosen by *Travel and Tourism* as "One of the Top 20 events in the Southeast." It features a horse parade through downtown, live entertainment, car shows, a farmers market and carnival rides.

Winston County has four sites on the National Register of Historic Places: Feldman's Department Store in Haleyville, the Houston Jail, the Winston County Courthouse in Double Springs and Archeological Site No. 1WI50 near Haleyville.

SWEET HOME ALABAMA

"Alabama" was written by Julia S. Tutwiler and composed by Edna Gockel Gussen. It became the official state song in 1931 and includes the lyrics:

"Alabama, Alabama, We will aye be true to thee,
From thy Southern shores where growth,
By the sea thy orange tree.
To thy Northern vale where floweth,
Deep blue the Tennessee,
Alabama, Alabama, we will aye by true to thee."

The southern rock band Lynyrd Skynyrd may have originated in Florida, but their signature hit "Sweet Home Alabama" is the rousing unofficial anthem of the state.

The lyrics (copyright Universal Music Publishing Group) include:

"Sweet home Alabama
Where the skies are so blue
Sweet home Alabama
Lord, I'm coming home to you
Here I come, Alabama"

"In Birmingham they love the Gov'nor . . . "

"Now Muscle Shoals has got the swampers
And they've been known to pick a song or two"

"Montgomery's got the answer"

Northwest Crossword

Solution on page 150.

Across

1. Weight lifting maneuver
5. Stylish
9. Alabama State Fair ewe or sow
12. Five Star Pizza hot spot
13. Marion County seat and hometown of former Alabama House of Representatives Speaker Rankin Fite
15. Bees' home
16. Physically unfit
17. Tharptown Elementary School addition word
18. Rice Box restaurant snakelike fish
20. Foaming at the mouth
21. "I had no ___!"
23. Young goat at the Colbert County Fair
25. Cousin of the gray wolf
28. Alabama county named in honor of the fifth U.S. President
30. Day before a holiday
32. Q-Tip
33. Melee
34. Alabama State Legislature staffer
36. Gist
37. Tennessee River town that is home to the Helen Keller Hospital
41. Drop the ball at a Muscle Shoals HS baseball game
44. On the Rocks gin flavor
45. Russellville Police Department traffic stopper
49. East Lawrence HS saxophonist's need
51. Huntsville jazz trumpeter Watters
52. Infuse with oxygen
53. Overage
55. Utter
57. University of North Alabama fraternity letters
58. Marion County Humane Society pound sound
59. Ryan's Barber Shop goo
61. Shoals Christian School baseball team single or double
62. Special time
66. WZDX-TV's *American* ___
68. Site of Heritage Christian University
69. Stubborn beast
70. Card below a jack at Wind Creek Casino
71. Edgemont Park picnic pests
72. Lawrence County Court jury member

Down

1. Frequent Franklin County Court "figure" (2 wds.)
2. Clear
3. Calvary Fellowship Church pastor, briefly
4. "Trick" joint
5. Old Chicago Cafe hot dog topper
6. Austin Manor B&B breakfast meat
7. Little devil
8. Cloak-and-dagger org.
9. Doesn't stick to the straight and narrow
10. Fiddler's gig
11. Stop
14. Burkes Brothers car with a bar
17. Looks at a target at Cedar Hill Trap Range
19. Barely make, with "out"
22. Liberal pursuits at UAB
24. Makes soundproof
25. Give up
26. UA sorority letter
27. Outward Gulf flow
29. Cries at the Tuscumbia fireworks

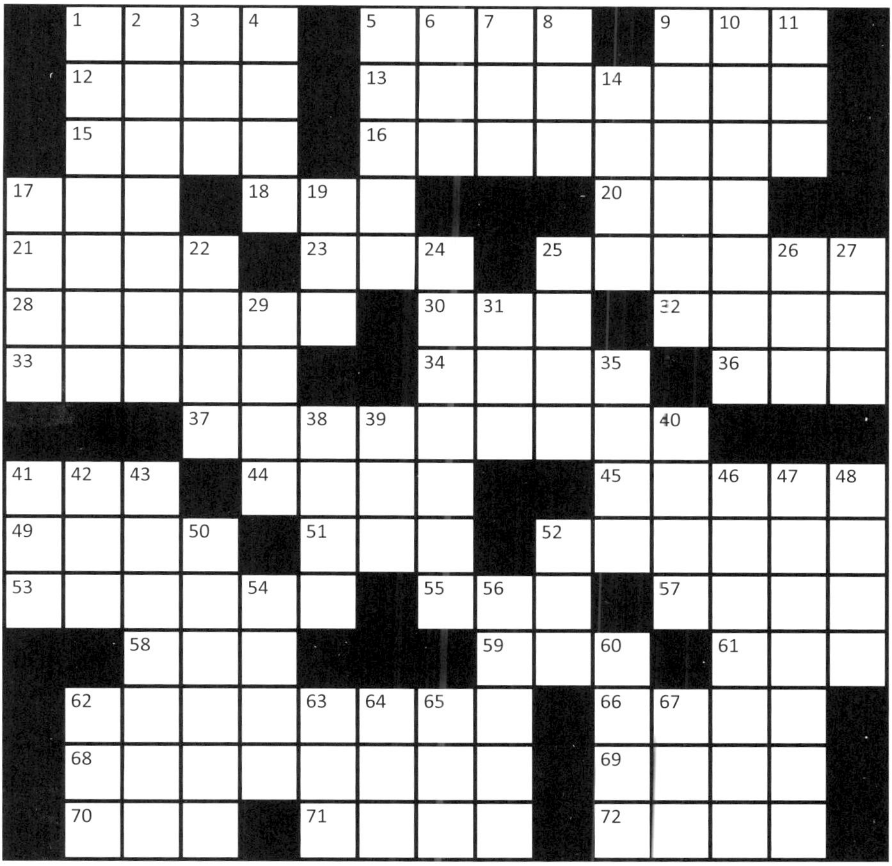

31. 7, in a Jacksonville State University Latin class
35. "If all ___ fails . . ."
38. Decatur lodge fellows
39. UNA Lions opponent
40. In ___ straits
41. Before, in verse
42. Morgan of the comics page
43. Go green
46. Small, dirty, uncomfortable place
47. Online merchant
48. Bankhead National Forest home
50. First Free Will Baptist Church official
52. Russellville City Council thumbs-up vote
54. Practice for an Alabama Golden Gloves bout
56. Redbox rental: ___ *of God*
60. Like a wet noodle
62. Frequently, in poetry
63. Caribbean, e.g.
64. Hampton or Budget follower
65. Alabama Renaissance Faire mo.
67. Word before date or process

Northwest Find the Words

Starting anywhere in the box, use adjacent letters—vertically, horizontally or diagonally—to make as many words as you can from the letters in SIPSEY WILDERNESS. Words need to be five or more letters and cannot use the same letter square more than once per word. No proper nouns, hyphenated or foreign words and no slang. We found 40 fairly common words, but there are 110 words that can be made that are in *The Official SCRABBLE Players Dictionary*. Find 30 words in 30 minutes to earn induction into the Solving Hall of Fame. List of words on page 151.

S	I	P	S
E	Y	W	I
L	D	E	R
N	E	S	S

1. ______________ 11. ______________ 21. ______________

2. ______________ 12. ______________ 22. ______________

3. ______________ 13. ______________ 23. ______________

4. ______________ 14. ______________ 24. ______________

5. ______________ 15. ______________ 25. ______________

6. ______________ 16. ______________ 26. ______________

7. ______________ 17. ______________ 27. ______________

8. ______________ 18. ______________ 28. ______________

9. ______________ 19. ______________ 29. ______________

10. ______________ 20. ______________ 30. ______________

Northwest Word Search

Solution on page 150.

V	H	O	D	G	E	S	G	R	U	B	W	E	N	L
T	H	G	I	R	W	L	W	I	N	F	I	E	L	D
Y	E	L	R	A	N	A	F	O	C	N	I	G	L	E
F	N	Z	E	A	N	O	T	L	I	M	A	H	E	D
M	I	D	W	A	Y	H	T	X	O	I	S	K	B	K
H	W	H	N	V	G	S	B	T	B	R	H	R	S	N
A	T	N	I	I	Z	E	O	M	A	T	E	D	I	A
L	Y	N	E	L	L	L	U	N	D	H	F	N	J	B
L	A	L	I	G	L	C	W	R	E	N	F	A	C	D
T	B	C	R	U	S	S	E	L	L	V	I	L	L	E
O	D	E	K	U	G	U	B	E	M	W	E	E	W	R
W	E	S	T	O	N	M	B	O	A	A	L	R	I	B
N	R	D	O	O	W	K	C	O	R	C	D	O	B	N
B	A	R	T	O	N	O	T	L	U	O	M	M	P	X

ADDISON	HILLSBORO	RED BAY
ARLEY	HODGES	ROCKWOOD
BARTON	ISBELL	RUSSELLVILLE
BELGREEN	KILLEN	SHEFFIELD
DELMAR	LEIGHTON	TUSCUMBIA
ELGIN	LYNN	TWIN
FLORENCE	MIDWAY	VINA
GRAYSON	MORELAND	WACO
GUIN	MOULTON	WESTON
HALLTOWN	MUSCLE SHOALS	WINFIELD
HAMILTON	NEWBURG	WREN
HATTON	RED BANK	WRIGHT

NORTHEAST

The Northeast region includes the major cities of Decatur, Huntsville and Gadsden.

Decatur (population 55,000) rose to prominence due to its location on Wheeler Lake along the Tennessee River and key railroad routes. Today, the city is known for its classic Victorian homes, as well as its chemical and aerospace companies. Attractions in "The River City" include Cook's Natural Science Museum, The Old State Bank (which dates to 1833), Point Mallard Park (a 750-acre recreation area on the Tennessee River) and the Wheeler National Wildlife Refuge (a 34,500-acre area that attracts migratory waterfowl).

Huntsville (population 180,000) is the birthplace of the U.S. space program. Spearheaded in 1950 by Dr. Wernher von Braun and a team of German scientists, the *Saturn V* moon rocket was developed there. NASA's George C. Marshall Space Flight Center later became instrumental in every aspect of the space program.

The U.S. Space and Rocket Center in Huntsville, Alabama is the most comprehensive U.S. manned space flight hardware museum in the world.

Huntsville is also home to Alabama Constitutional Village (the site where Alabama drew up the plan to join the Union), Burritt on the Mountain (an 11-room mansion in a historic park), Earlyworks Children's Museum (an interactive museum), Historic Huntsville Depot (a railroad museum featuring actual trains, as well as model trains), Huntsville Botanical Garden (a

120-acre plot), the Huntsville Museum of Art (featuring a wide variety of art), Sci-Quest (a hands-on learning experience), the U.S. Space and Rocket Center (an exploration center with an IMAX theater), Veterans Memorial Museum (with an exhibit with 30 military vehicles) and the Weeden House Museum (featuring furniture from the Federal period).

Gadsden (population 35,000) is located in the foothills of Lookout Mountain and local factories produce steel, rubber, fabricated metal, electrical equipment and electronic devices. Attractions include the Emma Sansom Monument (honoring the 15-year-old Alabama girl who guided Confederate General Nathan Bedford Forrest during the Civil War), the Gadsden Museum of Art (featuring a permanent collection of local and national artists as well as artifacts), the Mary G. Hardin Center for Cultural Arts (which includes the Imagination Place Children's Museum) and Noccalula Falls Park (that includes a 95-foot waterfall, an indoor-outdoor animal habitat, a war memorial, a train ride and botanical gardens).

Other highlights in the area are:

- Stevenson's Railroad Depot Museum.
- Athens' Veterans Museum and Archives.
- Cullman's Ave Maria Grotto (on the grounds of St. Barnard Abbey) and the County Museum.
- Hanceville's Evelyn Burrow Museum (that includes a 600-pound bronze double-mermaid fountain, Tiffany lamps, Faberge eggs and other sculptures.
- Attalla's Tigers for Tomorrow at Untamed Mountain (a 140-acre wildlife preserve that is home to more than 100 rescued big cats).
- Lake Guntersville (the state's largest lake at 69,000 acres, stretching more than 75 miles).
- Fort Payne's Alabama Fan Club and Museum (featuring memorabilia from the musical group Alabama), the Depot Museum and DeSoto State Park.

Bama Building Blocks

Read the clues and fill in the appropriate boxes, starting at the top. The answer to the second clue is the answer to the first clue, minus one letter. The answer to the third clue is the answer to the second clue, minus one letter, and so on. (The order of the letters may change.) Solution on page 151.

1. DeKalb County community two miles off State Route 75
2. Fairy tale meanies in a Scottsboro Public Library book
3. Candidate who got 41.6 percent of the Alabama vote in the 2000 U.S. Presidential election
4. Alabama mine find
5. Athens-Limestone Hospital surgical area, briefly
6. Letter on an Oneonta High School baseball cap

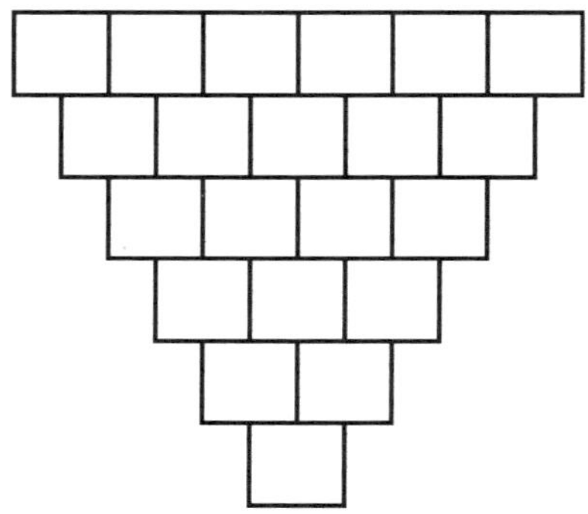

Decatur Wordsmith

Using the letters D-E-C-A-T-U-R, see how many words of four or more letters you can make. We found about 50 fairly common words (plus 32 more not so common ones that are acceptable in a game of SCRABBLE). Proper nouns, foreign words and abbreviations don't count. If you can find 40 or more words in 30 minutes, you're an All-State Wordsmith. Solution on page 151.

1. ____________ 15. ____________ 29. ____________
2. ____________ 16. ____________ 30. ____________
3. ____________ 17. ____________ 31. ____________
4. ____________ 18. ____________ 32. ____________
5. ____________ 19. ____________ 33. ____________
6. ____________ 20. ____________ 34. ____________
7. ____________ 21. ____________ 35. ____________
8. ____________ 22. ____________ 36. ____________
9. ____________ 23. ____________ 37. ____________
10. ____________ 24. ____________ 38. ____________
11. ____________ 25. ____________ 39. ____________
12. ____________ 26. ____________ 40. ____________
13. ____________ 27. ____________
14. ____________ 28. ____________

Northeast Crossword

Solution on page 151.

Across

1. The Buckeye State
5. Alabama Symphony Orchestra percussion instrument
9. Barely enough
14. Ivy League school
15. Iridescent gem at David's Jewelry
16. One of the Great Lakes
17. huntsvilleal.gov, e.g.
18. Nevada city
19. Most-wanted invitees
20. Housetop laborer
22. Reinvest, as winnings at Victoryland Greyhound Park
24. Marshall Space Flight Center org.
25. Headlight setting
26. 1972 Olympics swimming sensation, Mark ___
29. India Cafe wrap
32. Maxwell Air Force Base top guns
36. Arm bones in a UA anatomy class
37. Expected to arrive
38. Sitar Indian Cuisine bread
39. Word repeated in the lyric: "From ___ to shining ___"
40. City dubbed "Home of Meow Mix"
44. Big 10 Tires pressure init.
45. Put up in the Huntsville Museum of Art
47. Chop off
48. Propelled a boat in the Tennessee River
50. Brainchild
51. Auburn fraternity letter
53. Of service
54. URL part
56. Job for Joe Hudson's Collision Center
58. Wyoming's largest city
61. Modernize
64. Bamboo-munching critter
65. Competent
67. Starring role with the Bank Street Players
69. More suitable
70. Bit of dust
71. Use a surgical beam at Crestwood Medical Center
72. UAB basketball game score unit
73. Declaration at The Bridge Club of Huntsville
74. Final word at Beltline Church of Christ

Down

1. Gamestop purchase: "Call of Duty: Black ___"
2. Successor
3. Somerville Road Elementary School division word
4. Blount County seat and home to the Covered Bridge Festival
5. Tennessee political family
6. Ars Nova School of School of the Arts musical productions
7. A Bobbsey twin
8. Unappetizing school cafeteria serving
9. Puppeteer Lewis
10. City at Exit 308 on I-65
11. Highlight of 6-Down
12. Like a busybody
13. Charter Communications cable station
21. Disconcerted
23. Cafe Lemon Bleu farewell
26. Miyako Restaurant fare
27. Answer a charge in Jackson County Court
28. Asinine
30. Rework

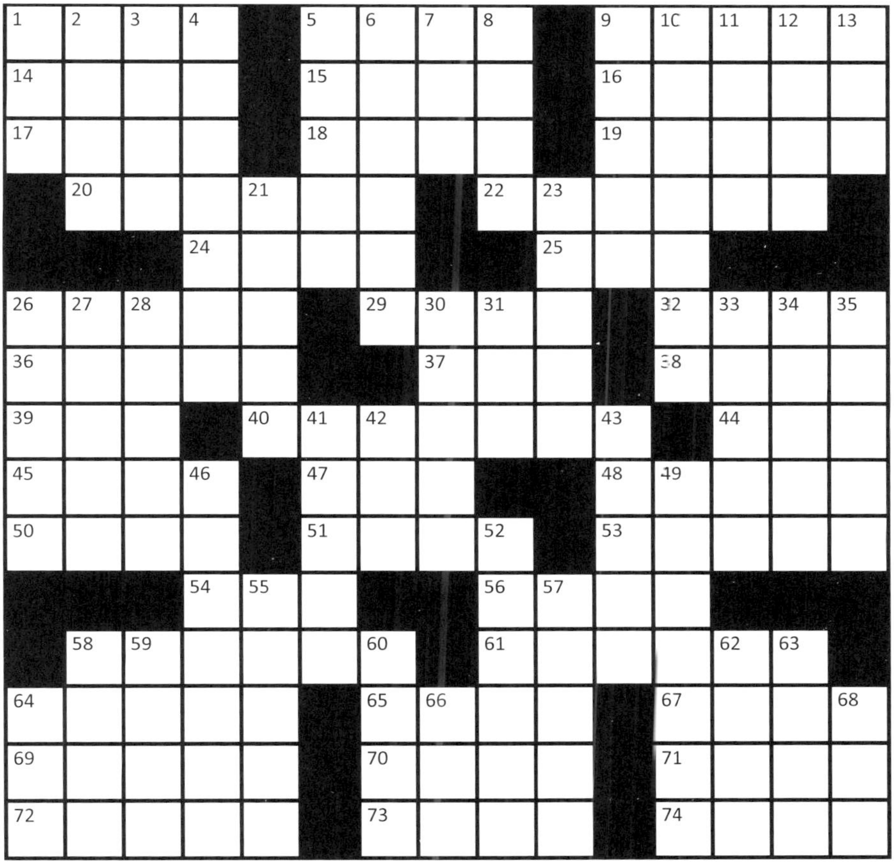

31. Same old, same old
33. Old Mercury at Huntsville Auto Auction
34. Supporter at the Carnegie Visual Art Center?
35. Said with a sneer
41. High society
42. Dove's sound
43. Mason's Pub order
46. Site of Noccalula Falls Park
49. Etowah County town whose seal reads: "Birthplace of Alabama Power"
52. Full-price payers at the EarlyWorks Children's Museum
55. Some abstract works at the BMA (2 wds.)
57. Huntsville Fencing Club swords
58. Mob boss
59. The A of ABM
60. I-65 exit
62. Eagles, Bearcats or Saints
63. "___ on Down the Road"
64. Drivel
66. Feathery wrap at Snickerpoodle Consignment Shop
68. Cub Scout Pack 188 group

Higdon Sudoku

Use logic to fill in the grid so every row, column and 2x3 box contains the letters H-I-G-D-O-N, in honor of the Jackson County community located at the top of Sand Mountain. Solution on page 152.

		O	N		
N	I			H	
				D	N
G	D				
	N			I	G
		D	H		

Baileyton Sudoku

Use logic to fill in the boxes so every row, column and 3x3 box contains the letters B-A-I-L-E-Y-T-O-N, in honor of the Cullman County town named after Robert Bailey, a farmer from Georgia. Solution on page 151.

				T	O	N		E
	B		I	N			T	
O						L		
				O	I		B	
I				A				Y
	O		Y	B				
		I						T
	N			I	B		L	
T		E	O	L				

CENTRAL WEST

Tuscaloosa and the University of Alabama dominate the Central West region.

Tuscaloosa (the fifth largest city in the state with a population of 90,000) is more than just a "campus town." The city was the state's capital from 1826-46. The university was founded in 1831.

Among the highlights of Tuscaloosa are the Battle-Friedman House (a Greek Revival mansion built in 1835), the Children's Hands-on Museum, the Tuscaloosa Museum of Art (featuring works by Winslow Homer, John Singer Sargent, James Whistler and Andrew Wyeth), the Alabama Museum of Natural History, the Gorgas House (built in 1829 as a student dining hall, and one of just four university buildings that survived the Civil War burning), the Black Warrior River, Stillman College (a historically black liberal arts school founded in 1876), Shelton State Community College (with an enrollment of 7,000 students), the Bama Theatre (1 1,094-seat proscenium theatre located downtown), the Tuscaloosa Symphony Orchestra, the Arboretum (a 60-acre garden with walking trails), Bryant-Denny Stadium (the UA football stadium that seats more than 100,000), Dreamland Bar-B-Que (founded by "Big Daddy" John Bishop in the Jerusalem Heights neighborhood), the Alabama Stage and Screen Hall of Fame and the Paul W. Bryant Museum (in honor of the long-time UA football coach).

Tuscaloosa is often referred to as the "Druid City" due to the numerous water oaks in the downtown area. A tornado in 2011 caused widespread destruction and killed 44 people in the city.

The least populous county in the state is Greene County with fewer than 9,000 residents. That equates to 15 people per square mile. Yet, the county still boasts nearly three dozen entries on the National Register of Historic Places, including the Gustave Braune House, the Capt. Nathan Carpenter Home, the First Presbyterian

Church (in Eutaw), and the Greene County Courthouse (built in 1868) at the Asa White House.

Other attractions in the region include the Fayette Art Museum (which features more than 3,500 works), Lake Tuscaloosa (a 5,885-acre reservoir that is popular for recreational activities), the first Mercedes-Benz assembly plant in the U.S. (located near Vance), Jasper's Downtown Historic District, the Alabama Mining Museum (in Dora), the Brierfield Furnace (the site of a former ironworks facility), the Centreville Historic District and the Moundville Archaeological Park (a Mississippian culture site that dates to 1000 AD).

Also: Lake Lurleen State Park (named in honor of former Gov. Lurleen Burns Wallace) near Tuscaloosa, the Kinterbish Wildlife Management Area (near Ward), the Tenn-Tom Waterway/Tom Bevill Visitor Center near Pickensville (a canal that connects the Tennessee River with the Tombigbee River and flows from the Gulf of Mexico to the nation's midsection), the Cochrane Recreation Area, the progressive Auburn University Rural Studio (a design-build architecture studio) and the Greensboro Historic District.

As well as: the eerie "face" etched in the window of the Pickens County Courthouse by a lightning bolt, the Aliceville Museum and Cultural Center (which houses artifacts from the Aliceville WWII POW camp), Aliceville Lake, Lamar (the birthplace of Rube Burrow, one of the most wanted outlaws of the 19th century after he committed a series of train robberies), Fayette's Ox Bodies (one of the world's leading producers of dump truck bodies), Bibb County (named after the first Governor of Alabama), the Cahaba River (which is home to the rare Cahaba Lily), West Blocton's beehive ovens (built in the late 1880s for coke production) and Northport's Kentuck Festival of the Arts.

MISSING H-A-L-E

Fill in the blanks with the letters H-A-L-E (for Hale County), once each, in any order, to form a fairly common six-letter word in each line. Solution on page 152.

1. __ __ I __ __ D
2. B __ __ __ __ F
3. __ __ R B __ __
4. __ __ __ __ T H
5. W __ __ __ T __
6. __ __ T __ __ R
7. __ __ __ V __ S
8. C __ __ __ __ T
9. __ W __ I __ __
10. __ __ S S __ __
11. W __ __ __ __ S
12. B __ __ __ C __

BONUS: There are only two six-letter words in an English dictionary that end with the letters H-A-L-E, in that order. The words are antonyms of each other, meaning that their definitions are opposites of each other. What are the words?

CENTRAL WEST FILL-IN

These Central West town names are listed in alphabetical order according to length. Fit them into their proper places in the Grid. We've started your solving by placing the town YORK. Now look for an 8-letter town name that has an O as the third letter. Continue working that way until you've filled in the Grid. But be careful. There might be a town that seems to work in more than one place, but each town is used just once. Solution on page 152.

5 Letters
AKRON
ASHBY
BRENT
CREWS
ELROD
GORDO
RALPH

6 Letters
ECHOLA
EMPIRE
HAMNER
KANSAS
LAWLEY
MARVEL
MCSHAN
PANOLA
REFORM
SIPSEY
WARSAW

7 Letters
BELMONT
BOLIGEE
CLINTON
COATOPA
FOSTERS
KENNEDY
MEMPHIS
STANSEL
STEWART

8 Letters
ELDRIDGE
FERNBANK
MILLPORT
PROSPECT
RANDOLPH

9 Letters
SARAGOSSA
SULLIGENT

Y O R K

Central West Crossword

Solution on page 152.

Across

1. Part of a Blossom Shop rose
5. Musician at the Alabama Renaissance Faire
11. Hidden means of support?
14. Domesticate an animal at the Birmingham Zoo
15. Spring bloomer in the UA Arboretum
16. Reel's partner at Orvis
17. Part 1 of final line of UA's fight song (2 wds.)
19. Bento Japanese Restaurant sash
20. Like a Bama winter, maybe
21. Redbox rental: *Raiders of the Lost ___*
22. Indian Hills Country Club prop
23. A deadly sin
26. 95.3 The Bear tune: "Better Than I Thought ___ Be"
28. Like most Northport streets
29. Time period in a UA geology class
30. Smell at Tuscaloosa's sewage treatment plant
32. Bank job
34. Light bulb unit
36. Alabama State Fair barn female
37. Ill temper
38. Part 2 of final line of UA's fight song (2 wds.)
43. Decay
44. Timberline Homes site
45. WBIQ-TV science show
47. Iguana Grill treats
49. Object of worship, like a UA gridiron star
51. Barely beat Georgia
52. DePalma's Italian Cafe plate
53. Finish, with "up"
54. Two under par at The Links at Tuscaloosa
56. End-of-list abbr.
57. Richmond Flowers Jr. to Richmond Sr.
59. Person Not Party fundraising org., for one
60. Twist the truth in Pickens County Court
61. Part 3 of final line of UA's fight song (2 wds.)
67. Holt Lake beachgoer's goal, often
68. Pantomime (2 wds.)
69. Mellow Mushroom pizzeria fixture
70. Rick-Bubba go-between
71. Central American pyramid builders
72. Tear apart

Down

1. Bama hog heaven?
2. Chinese ideal
3. Cousin of an ostrich
4. Kind of pay raise for a UA employee
5. Lord's mate
6. Israeli weapon
7. Alabama Department of Revenue assessment
8. Trojan War epic
9. Crystal ball user
10. Chore
11. Soup stocks at City Cafe
12. Former Obama press secretary Gibbs
13. "Farewell" in a Berry High School French class
18. Sound rebound
23. Use a needle at 1 Quick Fit Alteration
24. Panera Bread unit
25. "I'm ___ your tricks!"
26. Part of the Corn Belt
27. Morning glory aid

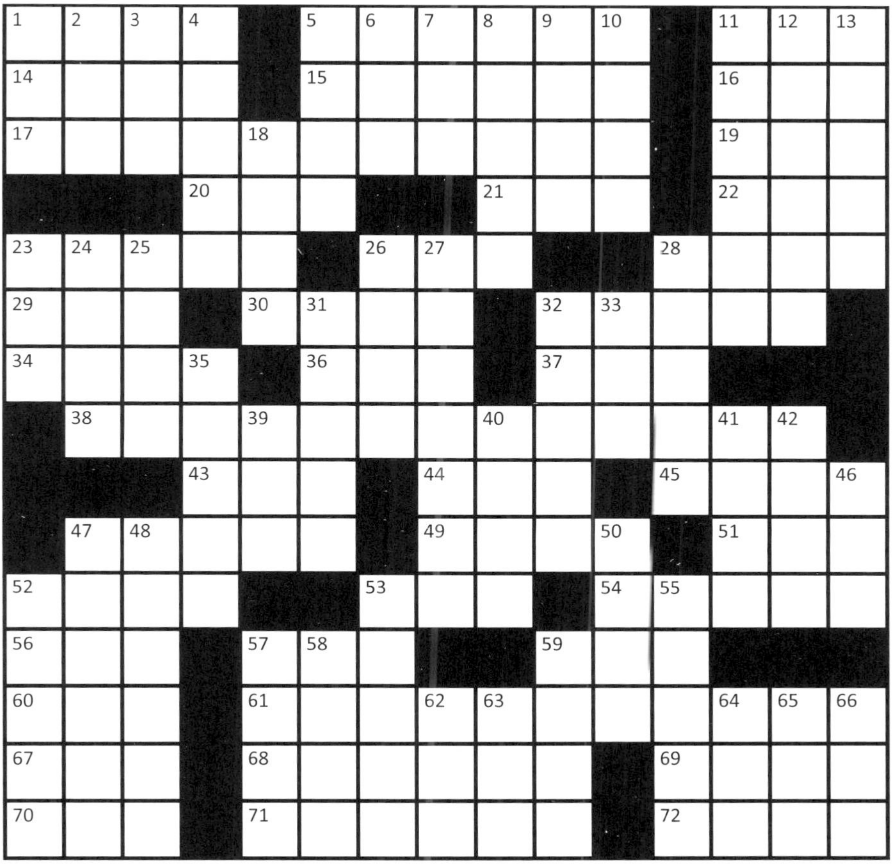

28. Link
31. Amounts in red numbers
32. Knowing what's what (2 wds.)
33. Be mistaken
35. Olympics symbol
39. *A Bridge ___ Far*
40. Alabama miner's quest
41. Denny Chimes sound
42. Wicked
46. Gulf Coast Zoo beast
47. One-named Italian painter represented at the Birmingham Museum of Art
48. Climb Cheaha Mountain
50. Like Jack Sprat's diet
52. Atlanta-based airline
53. Togetherness
55. George Lindsey or Michael Rooker, e.g.
57. Shell game
58. Killer whale
59. Black Rock Bistro kitchenware
62. Extinct flightless bird
63. WCFT-TV weather map symbol
64. ___ *Got a Secret*
65. TV room
66. You've just reached it

CENTRAL EAST

Birmingham is the largest city in Alabama with a population of 212,237. Its metro area has more than 1.1 million residents. With all those people come plenty of attractions and activities.

The Alabama Jazz Hall of Fame, located in the 1935 Carver Theatre for the Performing Arts, highlights the musical legends from Nat King Cole to Duke Ellington. The Alabama Sports Hall of Fame (located next to the city's convention complex) honors hundreds of athletes as well as displays of athletic achievement.

Other attractions include the Alabama Museum of the Health Sciences (on the campus of UAB), the Arlington Historic House and Gardens (a six-acre estate featuring a mansion furnished with 19th century decorative arts), the Birmingham Botanical Gardens (covering 68 acres with a variety of plants), the Birmingham Civil Rights Institute (a museum, research and education facility chronicling the local efforts), the Birmingham Museum of Art (with more than 24,000 pieces in its permanent collection), the Birmingham Zoo, the McWane Science Center (offering science adventures and interactive exhibits), the Ruffner Mountain Nature Center (a 1,000-acre forest and wildlife sanctuary), the Sixteenth Street Baptist Church (where four young women were killed by a bomb during the Civil Rights movement), the Sloss Furnaces National Historic Landmark (which dates to 1882), the Southern Museum of Flight and the Alabama Aviation Hall of Fame (presenting eight decades of history) and the Vulcan Park and Museum (featuring the 60-ton, 56-foot high Vulcan Statue, depicting the Roman god).

Also in the Central East region is the highest point in the state: Cheaha Mountain (elevation 2,407 feet) in the Talladega National Forest. The forest covers nearly 400,000 acres near the southern edge of the Appalachian Mountains.

Anniston (population 24,000) is the county seat of Calhoun County. Located on the slope of Blue Mountain, it was named The Model City in the late 19th century due to its careful planning. Today, the city seeks to preserve its history while becoming a bustling center of industry. The city is home to what was once recognized as the world's largest chair (at 31-feet tall) that stands next to Miller's Office Furniture. There is also the Berman Museum of World History, the Anniston Museum of Natural History, the Alabama Shakespeare Festival, the Alabama Symphony Orchestra's summer series of outdoor concerts, the nearby Anniston Army Depot and the Chief Ladiga Trail (90+ miles of paved rail trail for hikers and bikers).

Pelham is the site of Oak Mountain State Park, a 9,940-acre recreation area; Talladega is home to the Talladega Superspeedway (a 2.66-mile track that is the host of NASCAR races and the Dale Jarrett Racing School), as well as the International Motorsports Hall of Fame.

Pell City is on the shore of Lake Logan Martin; Munford is the location of the last battle of the Civil War east of the Mississippi River.

Oxford (which was originally named Lick Skillet) is a shopping mecca with the Quintard Mall and Oxford Exchange; Lincoln is home to a Honda manufacturing plant.

Calera was the fastest growing city in the state from 2000-2010, nearly quadrupling its population to 11,620; the city is home to the Heart of Dixie Railroad Museum and the historical Presbyterian Church.

Trussville was ranked No. 56 on *Money Magazine*'s list of the Best Places to Live. A canopy of stately trees lines downtown streets; a gazebo sits at the corner of Main Street and Parkway Drive. The Cahaba River is the city's symbol and plays an important role in the city's continued development.

Central East Crossword

Solution on page 152.

Across

1. Alabama Ballet attire
5. Hi-___ monitor
8. Olympics skiing event
14. Similar (to)
15. Alabama Fertility Specialists eggs
16. ’60s T-shirt coloring method at UAB
17. Birthplace of Bo Jackson
19. “One ___ Jump”
20. Bama Cowboy Saloon brew
21. Birmingham Zoo animal with a hump
23. Word after Hokes and Gorham’s in Alabama
26. Droops
27. Genesis son
31. Life of Riley
32. Too
33. Prefix with surgery or transmitter
34. Studio 21 Hair Salon coloring
35. Great Clips request
36. Alexandria HS volleyball position
37. Attention-getter
38. A bunch of
39. Neighbor of Croatia
42. Yours and mine
43. Amazement
46. Country Club of Birmingham clubs
47. Hanna’s Antique Mall LP player
48. Congeal, as blood
49. Jason’s sandwich shop
50. Game played on the Robert Trent Jones Trail
51. The German Club dance
52. Contemptuous look
54. Piggly Wiggly soup container
55. Defeated by the Blazers
58. City that was the inspiration for *Fried Green Tomatoes* (written by native Fannie Flagg)
63. Solvent
64. Gold’s, for one
65. Walkie-talkie word
66. Periods on jobs
67. Poseidon’s domain
68. Fortuneteller

Down

1. Frontera Bar & Grill bill
2. Island strings
3. “___ the season . . . ”
4. Risky
5. Alabama area that shares a name with a European capital
6. First lady
7. Humor that’s often lost in an e-mail
8. Itsy-bitsy bits in a Randolph County HS science class
9. Woe at the Shelby County animal shelter
10. Place with the ZIP codes 35054, 35125 and 35128 (2 wds.)
11. Bachelor’s last words
12. Big Apple inits.
13. *Birmingham News* comics shriek
18. Santa’s helper
22. In times past
23. Brookwood Medical Center unit
24. Winn-Dixie snack maker, Frito-___
25. Exploit
26. Built like a Miss Alabama contestant
28. Appear at The Whole Backstage
29. Intense anger
30. Postal motto word
32. 205: Birmingham’s ___ code
33. Macy’s department
35. Not that
36. Taj Indian wrap

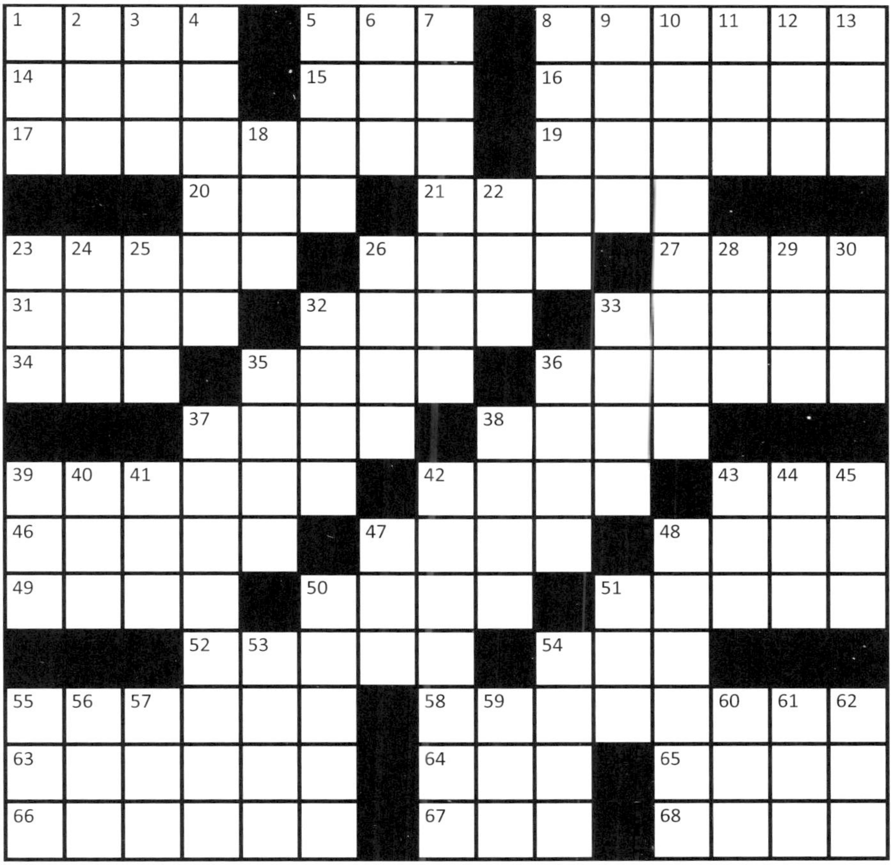

37. Calhoun County seat located on the slope of Blue Mountain
38. Fumble a punt for the Tide
39. Midfield Car Auction action
40. Wash. neighbor
41. Fa follower
42. Gulf fuel platforms (2 wds.)
43. Pledge of Allegiance ender
44. Shangri-La Restaurant kitchenware
45. BHM posting
47. Birmingham Botanical Gardens tool
48. *Pelham News* real estate ad section
50. Fellows
51. Kitchen need at John's City Diner
53. Straight, at Dram Whiskey Bar
54. Unwakable state
55. Some UAB undergrad degrees
56. Young newt
57. *Aladdin* prince
59. Bread at 49-Across
60. 5th or 6th, in Birmingham
61. Alabama author whose lone book won a Pulitzer Prize
62. Mess up

Malone Sudoku

Use logic to fill in the grid so every row, column and 2x3 box contains the letters M-A-L-O-N-E, in honor of the Randolph County community located just south of the Harris Dam at Lake Wedowee. Solution on page 153.

		M	N	O	
	O	A	L		
		E			
			E		
		N	M	L	
	M	L	O		

Muscadine Sudoku

Use logic to fill in the boxes so every row, column and 3x3 box contains the letters M-U-S-C-A-D-I-N-E in honor of the Cleburne County town that is just two miles from the Georgia border. Solution on page 153.

C		M					E	A
	I	E	U				N	
				E				C
			I		E		C	
		U		N		D		
	E		M		S			
E				S				
	N				D	C	M	
D	C					E		U

CENTRAL EAST WORD SEARCH

Solution on page 153.

M	A	H	A	R	G	O	I	S	I	C	L	A	C	M
A	L	M	O	N	D	O	O	W	E	M	O	H	A	U
H	Y	P	K	E	L	A	D	N	O	R	I	I	L	N
L	B	D	E	L	A	D	N	O	T	L	U	F	E	Y
E	L	L	E	L	A	D	N	E	D	R	A	G	R	B
P	E	E	K	I	L	A	G	E	D	A	L	L	A	T
I	H	I	U	V	U	C	R	E	B	N	X	N	B	L
N	S	F	D	S	K	S	I	E	R	N	W	E	D	I
S	A	R	Y	S	B	W	L	T	D	I	S	O	N	N
O	Y	A	G	U	A	C	A	L	Y	S	Y	R	A	C
N	R	B	R	R	K	L	V	H	E	T	D	F	L	O
A	E	G	L	T	A	B	P	M	N	O	O	N	G	L
D	E	T	N	O	M	D	E	I	P	N	O	E	A	N
O	X	F	O	R	D	R	O	F	N	U	M	R	R	B
S	N	I	L	L	O	H	A	T	L	E	D	J	T	Y

ABEL	CALCIS	HOLLINS	PIEDMONT
ADGER	CALERA	HOMEWOOD	PINSON
ALMOND	CHILDERSBURG	IRONDALE	RAGLAND
ALPINE	DELTA	LINCOLN	RENFROE
ANNISTON	DUKE	MOODY	SAYRE
ARGO	FULTONDALE	MUNFORD	SHELBY
BARFIELD	GARDENDALE	OXFORD	SYLACAUGA
BESSEMER	GRAHAM	PELHAM	TALLADEGA
BYNUM	HAWK	PELL CITY	TRUSSVILLE

MIDEAST

Montgomery has been the capital of Alabama since 1846. It was also the first capital of the Confederacy in 1861.

Representatives from seven states met in Montgomery to form the Confederate States of America; Jefferson Davis was sworn in as President on Feb. 18, 1861. (The capital was moved to Richmond, Va., on May 29, 1861.)

The city was captured by the Union on Apr. 12, 1865, three days after Gen. Robert E. Lee's surrender in Virginia and two days before President Lincoln was shot.

Montgomery may have given up its weapons, but it did not give up its convictions. The South began rebuilding—its buildings and way of life.

In the mid-20th century, the city was in the midst of the African-American Civil Rights Movement: Rosa Parks refused to give up her seat on a bus in 1955, Martin Luther King Jr. was a pastor of a local Baptist church, mob violence took place at the Greyhound Bus Station, and Gov. George Wallace was fighting the end of segregation from his office in the capitol.

Today, Montgomery (population 205,000) is the second largest city in the state, but still displays its Southern charms and lifestyle. Attractions in addition to the State Capitol include the Alabama Shakespeare Festival, Alabama War Memorial, the Civil Rights Memorial Center, the Dexter Avenue King Memorial Baptist Church, the Hank Williams Museum, the Mann Wildlife Learning Museum, the Montgomery Museum of Fine Arts, the Montgomery Zoo, the MOOseum, the Old Alabama Town, St. John's Episcopal Church, the Scott and Zelda Fitzgerald Museum, the State Archives and History Museum and the Troy University Rosa Parks Museum.

Other places of note in the 12-county region are: Tuskegee, Auburn, Opelika and Lake Martin.

Tuskegee (population 12,000) is home to the famed institute founded by Booker T. Washington and where the Tuskegee Airmen trained.

Auburn (population 53,000) is the site of Auburn University and is dubbed "The Loveliest Village On The Plains." *U.S. News & World Report* named Auburn as one of the 10 best places to live in the U.S. in 2009. Tourist spots include the Auburn University Chapel, Old Main, the Jonathan B. Lovelace Hall of Honor, the Jule Collins Smith Museum of Fine Arts and nearby Chewacla State Park.

Opelika (population 26,000) is known for its Azalea/Dogwood Trail that showcases several Victorian homes and the Museum of East Alabama (which has more than 10,000 items chronicling the history of the state, the region and the city).

Lake Martin was formed in 1926 with the completion of the Martin Dam. At the time, it was the largest man-made body of water in the world. Today, it is 44,000 acres with 750 miles of wooded shoreline. Activities in the area include boating, fishing, water skiing, swimming, camping, hiking and golfing.

Other highlights include:

- Selma (population 20,000) is rich in Civil War and Civil Rights history, in addition to being home to the Old Cahawba Archaeological Park, the Old Depot Museum, Sturdivant Hall and the Vaughn-Smitherman Museum.
- Clanton (population 8,600) is the county seat of Chilton County and the site of a World War II POW camp and an annual Peach Festival.
- Alexander City (population 14,800) points of interest include Central Alabama Community College, the Reuben Herzfeld House, the Avondale Historic District and the First United Methodist Church.
- The Paul M. Grist State Park, which is located on the southern edge of the Talladega National Forest in Dallas County.

MIDEAST CROSSWORD

Solution on page 153.

Across

1. Good name for a Dalmatian
5. More despicable
10. Iridescent gem at Rosen Jewelry
14. Scott Street Deli sandwich
15. Bring to mind
16. Cuco's Mexican Cafe coin
17. Black-and-white treat from Winn-Dixie
18. Matched
19. Redbox rental: ___ *Brockovich*
20. Lionel Richie's hometown
22. Chisholm Park playground feature
23. Bone-dry
24. Unread part of a *Montgomery Advertiser* movie review, maybe
26. Kind of skates at Goodwill
29. Use one's head at Auburn University
30. Hurts badly
31. Montgomery Biscuits pitchers' stats
32. St. Peter Catholic Church vestments
36. Cypress Tree Golf Course instructor
37. Like a straw
40. Sterling Bank offering, for short
41. Harmony
43. Centre newspaper: *The* ___
44. Montgomery high-rise construction girder
46. Lake Harding "crazy" birds
48. Uptight (2 wds.)
49. Resembling a Lanett HS third-string player, maybe
52. Kathryn C. Thornton's org. with a mission
53. Biblical possessive
54. Montgomery County town that grew from 310 residents in 2000 to more than 5,000 in 2010 (2 wds.)
58. Tallapoosa River floater
59. ThyssenKrupp alloy
61. The Dansby Law Firm assignment
62. Norse capital
63. '60s "V" sign at Auburn University
64. Vicinity
65. Hammer part
66. Part of a court at O'Connor Tennis Center
67. Peter the Great, e.g.

Down

1. Tried to score at Auburn Arena
2. Lima's land
3. Alabama mine finds
4. Lined up the cross hairs at Tri-County Shooting Range (2 wds.)
5. Corn or potato at the Alexander City Farmers Market
6. Like some Troy University campus walls
7. Brain section
8. Barely get, with "out"
9. Robert E. Lee HS color
10. Home of the renowned Robert Trent Jones Grand National golf course
11. Danger
12. Comment to the audience at the Alabama Shakespeare Festival
13. Recluse
21. Young's accounting partner
22. "My boy"
24. Ten Commandments word
25. Leaning tower city

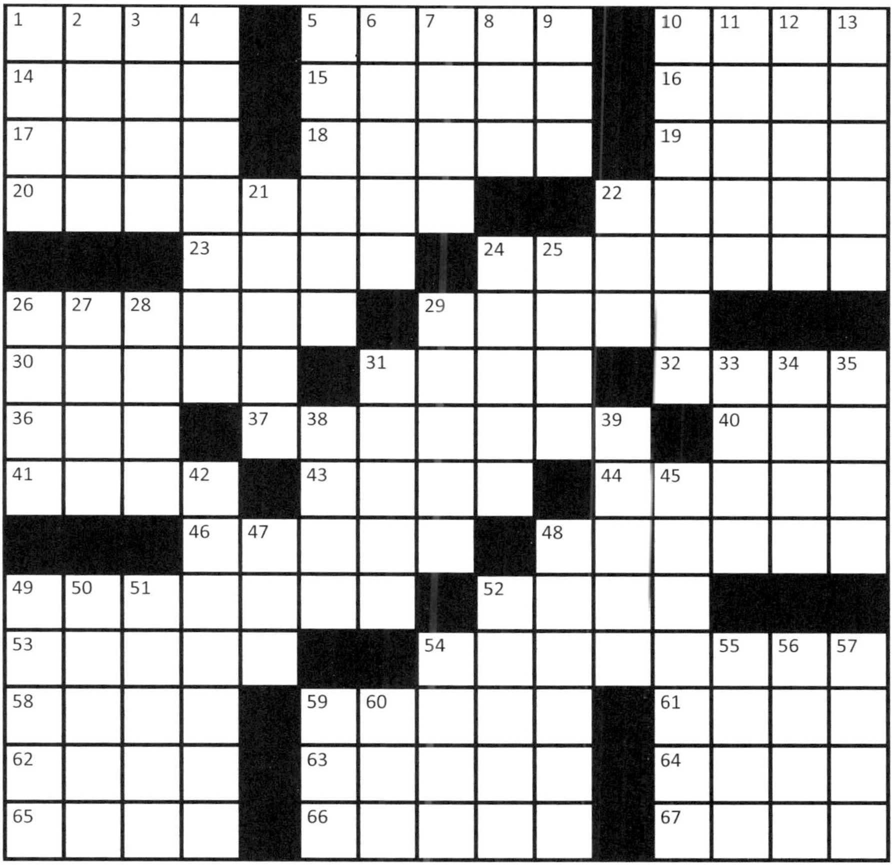

26. Little devils
27. ___ a soul
28. Birmingham Zoo pride member
29. Edmund Pettus Bridge support
31. Piano key material at Art's Music Shop
33. Served up a whopper
34. Crow about a Tigers win
35. Ditto
38. "Once ___ a time . . ."
39. Family Laundry washer cycle
42. Chilton County seat named after a Confederate Army general
45. Cullman HS or Weaver HS athlete
47. Be in debt to Regions Bank
48. Sharpshooting Annie
49. Razor sharpener at Heritage Barber Shop
50. Selma bank
51. The R in NRA
52. Family reunion attendee
54. Samford Hall bell tower ring
55. Auburn Rowing Club equipment
56. Fishing in the Gulf, perhaps
57. Letter opener
59. Seaborn Salon, e.g.
60. No. on a Rheem business card

Opelika Wordsmith

Using the letters O-P-E-L-I-K-A, see how many words of four or more letters you can make. We found about 20 fairly common words (plus 17 more not so common ones that are acceptable in a game of SCRABBLE). Proper nouns, foreign words and abbreviations don't count. If you can find 15 or more words in 15 minutes, you're an All-Pro Wordsmith. Solution on page 153.

1. ________________
2. ________________
3. ________________
4. ________________
5. ________________
6. ________________
7. ________________
8. ________________
9. ________________
10. ________________
11. ________________
12. ________________
13. ________________
14. ________________
15. ________________

THE ONE AND ONLY ONE ROBA

Find the one and only complete ROBA in the grid, in honor of the Macon County community. It might run forward or backward, up or down or diagonally. Solution on page 154.

R B O A O R R B A O R O B O R

O B A R B O A R O B B O R A O

B A O R O A B O O B R O B R B

R O B B A O R B B A R A B R O

R O B B R R O B O R B O R B A

O B A R O B O B A R O B B A O

R B O A A A B B B O O O R R R

O R B A R B B O O R O O B O O

B O O R B A R B O A B R A B R

O R B A B O B A A A B O A O A

R A B A B B O A A R B O O B R

O A B B A R R A O O B A B O B

B R O R R A R R A R O R O A O

R A B O O R B A O R R B A R O

O R O A O B A O B A O R B O R

Gulf Coast

The Alabama Gulf Coast is the state's gateway to the Gulf of Mexico. Mobile Bay's mouth is formed by the Fort Morgan Peninsula on the east and Dauphin Island on the west. It is fed on the north by the Mobile River and Tensaw River. The Bay is 413 square miles, making it the fourth largest estuary in the U.S. The average depth is 10 feet, but the shipping channel is more than 75 feet deep.

The Port of Mobile is the ninth largest in the nation with a trade volume of more than 65 million tons. The primary cargo going through the Port is forest products and coal.

The major city on the Bay is Mobile (population 195,000). Attractions include the Mobile Mardi Gras (said to be the first in the U.S.), the Festival of Flowers (held every March), the Bayfest Music Festival (held every October), Bienville Square (a downtown park), the Bragg-Mitchell Mansion (a combination of Greek Revival and Italianate), the Cathedral of the Immaculate Conception (built in 1850), the Conde-Charlotte Museum House (Mobile's first jail and courthouse dating to 1822), Fort Conde (from the Louisiana Territory days, it now serves as the city's official welcome center), the Gulf Coast Exploreum Science Center (featuring more than 150 interactive displays), the Mobile Botanical Gardens (a 100-acre site), Mobile Medical Museum (exhibiting artifacts from the late 1700s), the Mobile Museum of Art (with a permanent collection of 6,000 works), Mobile's Historic Districts (a cross section of the local architectural heritage), The Museum of Mobile (presenting more than 300 years of history), the National African-American Archives & Multicultural Museum (which houses biographies of significant African-Americans), the Oakleigh Historic Complex (a dual museum), the Phoenix Fire Museum (with relics from former fire stations), the Richard Dar House (built in 1860), the Soldiers and Sailors Memorial Park (in honor of the soldiers killed in World

War I) and the USS *Alabama* Battleship Memorial Park (dedicated to the Alabamans who served in the military).

Other highlights along the coast are Gulf Shores (home of the Alabama Gulf Coast Zoo, the Bon Secour National Wildlife Refuge, Fort Morgan State Historic Site, the Gulf Shores Museum and Waterville USA), Spanish Fort (the site of a longtime fort, Historic Blakeley State Park and Meaher State Park), Daphne (home to the U.S. Sports Academy, Bayfront Park, American Sport Art Museum and Archives and the Malbis Memorial Church), Fairhope (a resort city with lots of unique art, shops and yachting) and Orange Beach (a coastal town near Gulf State Park and home to the tallest Ferris wheel in the Southeast).

Gulf Shores is known for its bright, "sugar white" quartz sand.

Some of the major attractions inland include: Monroeville (hometown of authors Truman Capote and Harper Lee and home of the Monroe County Courthouse Museum), the Millers Ferry Dam (that creates the 27-square mile William "Bill" Dannelly Reservoir), Thomaston (site of the Alabama Rural Heritage Center), Linden (three miles south of Chickasaw State Park) and Demopolis (site of Christmas in the Cranebrake, Christmas on the River, Harvest Festival and the Southern Literary Trail).

Also: Mount Sterling (home to a historic Methodist Church built in 1859), McIntosh (site of Andrews Chapel), and St. Stephens (home of the Old Washington County Courthouse and Old St. Stephens Site).

Made in Mobile

Several movies have been shot or have been set in Mobile. Here are some of those flicks. Match the film with the star. Solution on page 154.

1. *Close Encounters of the Third Kind* (1977)
2. *Back Roads* (1981)
3. *Raw Nerve* (1991)
4. *Stone Cold* (1991)
5. *Night Trap* (1993)
6. *Raw Justice* (1994)
7. *Executive Decision* (1996)
8. *Love Liza* (2002)
9. *Mi Amigo* (2002)
10. *The Final Destination* (2009)

a. Pamela Anderson

b. Brian Bosworth

c. Bobby Camp

d. Robert Davi

e. Richard Dreyfuss

f. Sally Field

g. Glenn Ford

h. Philip Seymour Hoffman

i. Josh Holloway

j. Kurt Russell

Gulf Coast If . . . Then

Complete this puzzle to reveal an annual Mobile attraction. Solution on page 154.

___ ___ ___ ___ ___ ___   ___ ___ ___ ___
1 2 3 4 5 6   7 8 9 10

* If the annual National Shrimp Festival is held in Gulf Shores, then the 8th letter is O; if it is in Florence, then the 2nd letter is U.
* If the USS *Alabama* battleship is docked in Mobile, then the 3rd letter is N; if it is the USS *Tuskegee*, then the 9th letter is M.
* If the town at I-10, Exit 4 is Summerdale, then the 6th letter is M; if it is Grand Bay, then the 10th letter is L.
* If the code for the Birmingham-Shuttlesworth International Airport is BSA, then the 7th letter is G; if it is BHM, then the 5th letter is O.
* If Montgomery is named after Revolutionary War General Richard Montgomery, then the 2nd letter is R; if it is the French explorer Pierre Mont Gomere, then the 1st letter is M.
* If Huntsville is in Monroe County, then the 4th letter is E; if it is Madison County, then the 6th letter is R.
* If Auburn University was founded by a group of Catholic priests, then the 5th letter is U; if it was a group of Methodists, then the 9th letter is W.
* If Tuscaloosa is south of Atlanta, then the 4th letter is I; if it is north, then the 10th letter is E.
* If Decatur is on Lake Black Creek, then the 8th letter is A; if it is Wheeler Lake, then the 1st letter is S.
* If Dothan has a higher elevation than Gadsden, then the 3rd letter is S; if it is lower, then the 7th letter is B.

Gulf Coast Crossword

Solution on page 154.

Across

1. Part of an Appalachian jug band
4. Telephoned
8. Auth. unknown
12. Wise one
13. Alabama polecat's defense
14. Goofy
15. Longtime 1st District rep in the U.S. House, ___ Callahan
16. Toys"R"Us building blocks
17. Fable
18. Women of the Archdiocese of Mobile
19. Matterhorn, e.g.
20. Lab eggs
22. "___ to Billie Joe"
23. Dundee denizen
24. County that contains the communities of Frisco City, Excel and Burnt Corn
28. County named after a U.S. Senator from Georgia
30. Redbox rental: *A ___ Good Men*
31. Century 21 competitor
32. Fizzle
33. Scoundrel
34. Afternoon socials at a plantation
35. Sir's mate
38. Spencer Elementary School lad
39. Like much of east central Alabama
40. Not home in Mobile
41. Recite
42. Ornamental bloom at Bay Flowers
43. Go bad
44. 007, for one
45. County that includes the Faunsdale Plantation and Confederate Park
49. County that is home to Fort Sinquefield
51. Lincoln's coin
52. Chatter on and on
53. Exxon lubricant
54. Washington's bill
55. Fairhope HS color
56. Gulf Shores St. crossers
59. Mardi Gras follower
61. Resembling *Playboy* Playmate Angela Little's tresses
62. Fuzzy fruit
63. Descartes' "therefore"
64. Jemima, e.g.
65. Call from the flock at Cottage Hill Baptist Church
66. Kind of admiral
67. Mins. and mins.

Down

1. Mobile's Bankhead ___
2. Radney Funeral Home ashes holders
3. Edward Jones stock order
4. CVS deodorant type
5. Proficient
6. Yule quaff
7. Neatened up Rover's appearance at Adorable Do's
8. Jingle writer for WBHY radio, maybe
9. Jackson City Council no vote
10. Frequently, in verse
11. Utmost degree
12. Foley Cheese Shop purchase
15. One whose nose is in the air
19. Advance Auto Parts battery fluid
21. Solemn promise
23. Having dogpaddled in the Tensaw River
25. Carmike Cinema's film unit
26. University of South Alabama face-to-face exam
27. "No problem!"
29. Time to act
30. Wray of *King Kong*

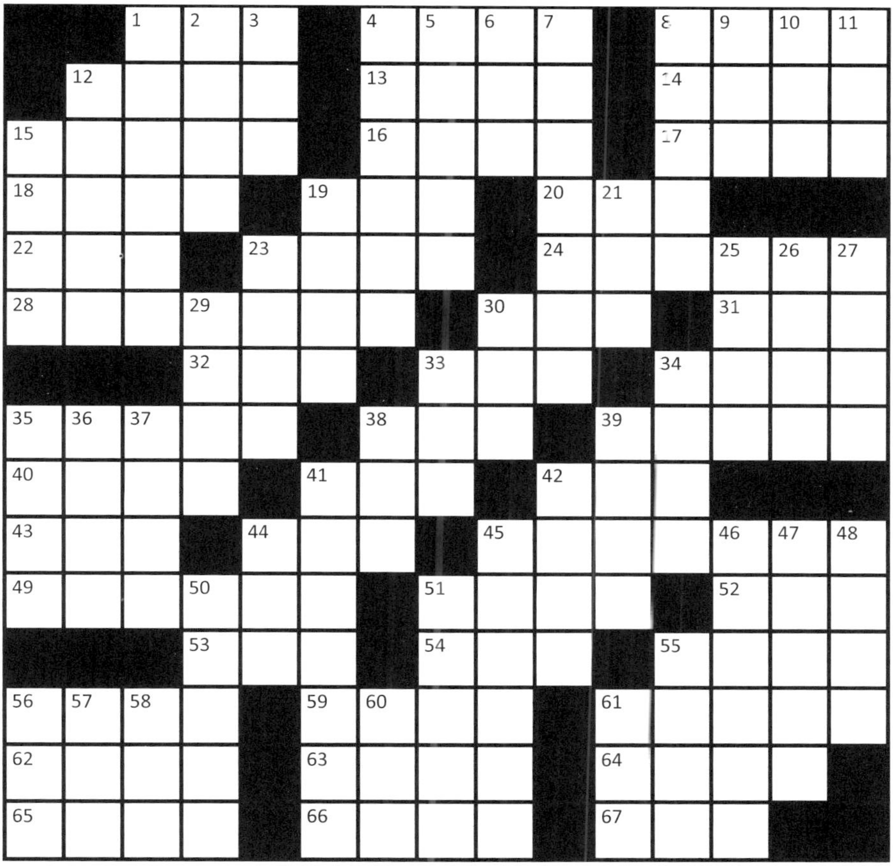

33. Artfully shy
34. Part of CDT
35. Painter Chagall
36. Missing from the Mobile Coast Guard Aviation Training Center
37. Facts and figures
38. Where one's ship may come in: Mobile ___
39. In pain
41. Bee participant
42. Locks in a Delta Downs barn?
44. Word with water or jet in Gulf Shores
45. Personal counselor
46. Hose
47. All skin and bones
48. *Thomasville Times* page
50. Hank Aaron Stadium pitcher's bagful
51. Line dance
55. Fuzzy image
56. Alabama Highway Patrol blotter letters
57. Vigor go-with
58. Randall Farms female
60. Alabama Poet Laureate preposition
61. "___, humbug!"

Butler Sudoku

Use logic to fill in the grid so every row, column and 2x3 box contains the letters B-U-T-L-E-R, in honor of the county seat of Choctaw County that is the hometown of country music singer Ty Herndon. Solution on page 154.

U					
	T	B	R		L
B		R	L		
		U	B		E
R		E	U	L	
					R

Gulf Crest Sudoku

Use logic to fill in the boxes so every row, column and 3x3 box contains the letters G-U-L-F-C-R-E-S-T, in honor of the village in Mobile County that is located on U.S. Route 45. Solution on page 154.

R					G		T	
		C		U	F		E	R
		S	R	E		G		F
U			L		C	F	R	E
				T				
C	R	F	U		E			G
F		U		R	S	L		
S	C		G	L		E		
	G		C					S

Southeast

The Southeast region of Alabama is bordered by Florida on the south and Georgia on the east.

The major city in the region is Dothan (population 65,000), which is located 20 miles west of Georgia and 18 miles north of Florida. Known as "The Peanut Capital of the World," Dothan and nearby communities account for about a quarter of all the peanuts processed in the U.S. The city became the county seat of Houston County in 1903 and is home to the George Washington Carver Museum and Monument, the Wiregrass Museum of Art, the Peanut Monument, the Southeast Alabama Community Theater, the "Joseph" Statue in Millennium Park (depicting the Bible verse: "For I heard them say, Let us go to Dothan" Genesis 37:17), the Opera House (built in 1915), the Botanical Gardens and the Wiregrass Festival of Murals.

Peanuts have played an important role in southern Alabama agriculture since they were brought to the U.S. by African slaves. The peanut plant is part of the legume family. It grows to just over a foot in height. Once the plant's flowers wilt, the stalk grows down into the ground and develops pods containing the seeds (nuts). When the seeds mature, they are ready for harvest, usually in September or October.

The state ranks third in peanut production in the U.S. behind Georgia and Texas. More than 400 million pounds of peanuts are harvested annually in Alabama on about 200,000 acres. Dothan's annual Peanut Festival attracts more than 100,000 visitors to the area.

Nearby is Fort Rucker. The U.S. Army post was named for Confederate General Edmund Rucker and covers more than 58,000 acres. Opened in 1942, it is primarily a flight training base for Army Aviation, as well as the home of the U.S. Army Aviation Center of Excellence and the U.S. Army Aviation Museum.

The post has three operational units: the 1st Aviation Brigade, the 110th Aviation Brigade and the USAF 23rd Flying Training Squadron for the training of Air Force helicopter pilots.

Its mission statement is: "The U.S. Army Aviation Center of Excellence trains military, civilian, and international personnel in aviation and leadership skills, integrates Army aviation warfighting doctrine and requirements determination across the DOTMLPF, manages available resources, and sustains our commitment to the well-being of our Soldiers, civilians, retirees, and Families."

The Army Aviation Museum has a collection of more than 150 military aircraft, including one of the largest collections of military helicopters in the world. Displays chronicle the beginning of flight with the Wright brothers to early combat planes from World War I to modern flying military aircraft.

Other attractions are the Boll Weevil Monument at Enterprise; Opp, "The City of OPPortunity"; Andalusia, the site of the annual World Championship Domino Tournament; Troy University and the University Arboretum at Troy; site where the first female pilot in the U.S. Navy, Barbara Allen Rainey, crashed and died in 1982, near Evergreen; and Greenville, the home of the Watermelon Jubilee, the Old Time Farm Day, Sherling Lake Park and Campground and the Ritz Theatre.

Also: Atmore's Rivercane development, a 740-acre missed-use development off I-65, Old-Time Fiddlers' Convention, Poarch Creek Indian Pow-wow, Mayfest and William Station Day; Geneva's Constitution Oak along the Choctawhatchee River, believed to be the oldest living oak in the state; Abbeville's Atlantic Coast Line Railroad Depot, the Archie Theatre and the Bethune-Kennedy House; Eufaula's National Wildlife Refuge, First United Methodist Church, the Shorter Mansion and Fendall Hall; and Phenix City's Morgan-Curtis House and Brooks-Hughes Home.

COMPLETE THE 'VILLES

The southeast corner of Alabama is loaded with communities that end in –VILLE. Complete the names of these towns by using each of the 24 letters listed once. Solution on page 155.

A B C D E F G H I J K L

M N O P R S T U V W X Y

1. ___ R E E ___ ___ N V I L L E

2. ___ I ___ O N ___ I L L E

3. ___ O ___ N S ___ N V I L L E

4. ___ ___ E ___ N V I L L E

5. L I ___ E R ___ ___ V I L L E

6. ___ O ___ ___ S V I L L E

7. ___ ___ I P ___ E R V I L L E

8. L A ___ R E ___ ___ E V I L L E

Southeast Crossword

Solution on page 155.

Across

1. Ruler unit at Troy Elementary School
5. Drop a fly ball at Riverwalk Stadium
9. PoFolks Restaurant plate
13. Truth or ___ (UAB sorority game)
14. On a boat in the Gulf
15. Cowboy games
16. Conecuh County seat named after a fir
18. Alabama A&M first-stringers
19. Repair a tear at Lani's Tailor
20. Help for a Pittsview pedestrian
21. Get some air
22. In ___ of (replacing)
23. Swipes second for the Enterprise HS baseball team
24. Perspire at Gold's Gym
27. Undo, as laces
29. Italian public square
31. Smoke House Billiard Parlor stick
32. J. Edgar Hoover's org.
35. Pseudo-cultured
36. Gulf wave
38. Kind of piper
39. "Absolutely!"
40. Caribbean, e.g.
41. Like most Hawaiian shirts
43. Fancies up
46. Scrumptious at Huggin' Molly's Restaurant
47. Ready for harvest at Scotts Orchard
49. The Beatles' "Back in the ___"
51. Carroll HS football player's protection
52. A fan of the Crimson Tide
53. Death on the Nile cause, perhaps
56. Numbskull
57. Site of the annual World Championship Domino Tournament
59. Rolens Bakery cake layers
60. A long way off, like Alaska
61. Performed for the Birmingham Children's Choir
62. Fit to be tried in the Pike County Court
63. Bellingrath Gardens weeder
64. St. Theresa Catholic Church area

Down

1. Bad day for Caesar
2. Cathedral of St. Paul section
3. UA rowing team
4. Redbox rental: *Death Becomes ___*
5. Monroeville's "Fruitcake Lady" Rudisill
6. Beneficial
7. Talladega Speedway pedal pushers
8. Auburn Tigers groupie
9. Houston County town named after a Genesis location
10. Consummate
11. Navy elite
12. Instruction to a Southern Comfort Limousine driver
15. Rajah's wife
17. Sparkle
21. In and of ___
22. Having no get-up-and-go
23. CD Warehouse music genre
24. Neuter at the Coffee County humane society
25. Telegram
26. Chows down at Willy T's Chicken Fingers

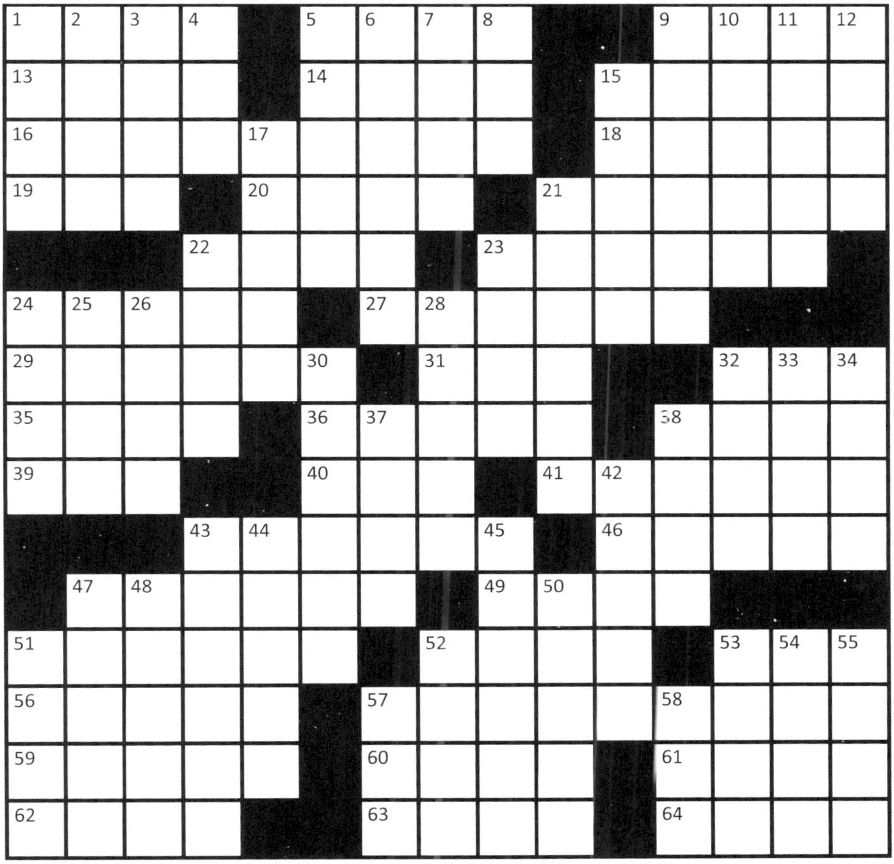

28. Blue part of a map in an Elba HS geography class
30. Classify
32. Al dente at Milano Ristorante
33. Laser light
34. One way to stand by
37. Bama fans chant: "___ number one!"
38. Rain hard
42. Kroger disinfectant brand
43. Home of the annual Old-Time Fiddlers' Convention and the Poarch Creek Indian Pow-wow
44. The Blind Boys of Alabama 2009 album name
45. Dairy Queen order
47. *The Southeast Sun,* WPMI-TV and WAPR, et al.
48. Extraterrestrial
50. Former UA quarterback, Bart ___
51. Q-94 chart-topping songs
52. Data
53. Quickly, in a Shaw Industries memo
54. Breaks a commandment
55. Young aide in the Alabama State Legislature
57. Ooh and ___
58. Mobile campus, briefly

SOUTHEAST WORD SEARCH

Solution on page 155.

U	C	H	E	E	U	F	A	U	L	A	V	O	N	R
R	E	I	Z	O	D	U	K	I	N	S	E	Y	J	N
B	H	N	A	I	S	U	L	A	D	N	A	D	O	E
L	S	T	T	A	R	P	I	A	T	E	N	O	N	Q
A	W	P	K	E	E	G	O	B	R	E	W	T	O	N
C	E	E	H	U	R	T	S	B	O	R	O	H	T	P
K	U	Z	L	O	P	P	S	E	Y	G	C	A	Y	S
N	X	E	E	L	E	Q	R	V	T	R	V	N	A	K
P	S	G	Y	T	I	C	X	I	N	E	H	P	L	O
H	P	E	N	R	E	V	U	L	S	V	E	O	C	O
A	E	M	A	R	L	F	N	L	G	E	O	Z	B	R
C	R	N	O	L	R	O	Y	E	L	T	N	A	R	B
O	O	M	C	K	E	N	Z	I	E	O	Z	R	Y	E
D	T	X	C	M	A	S	H	F	O	R	D	K	R	C
A	E	D	W	I	N	U	J	L	X	C	G	X	Q	K

ABBEVILLE
ANDALUSIA
ASHFORD
ATMORE
AVON
BECK
BLACK
BRANTLEY
BREWTON
BROOKS
CLAYTON
DOTHAN
DOZIER
EDWIN
ENON
ENTERPRISE
EODA
EUFAULA
EVERGREEN
GEORGIANA
GREENVILLE
HACODA
HURTSBORO
KEEGO
KINSEY
LUVERNE
MARL
MCKENZIE
OPP
OZARK
PEROTE
PHENIX CITY
PRATTS
SEALE
TROY
UCHEE

Part III: Alabama Activities

ARTS & ENTERTAINMENT

Alabama residents are well aware of the many cultural activities available throughout the state.

Lovers of live theatre can be entertained by Alabama's Official Outdoor State Drama, "The Miracle Worker" (about the life of Helen Keller), staged every year in Tuscumbia. "The Incident at Looney's Tavern" (about a meeting during the opening stages of the Civil War) is the state's Official Musical Drama, performed annually in Winston County. There are more than 30 theater companies in Alabama.

Dance fans enjoy everything from ballet to folk. The Alabama Ballet Company is based in Birmingham; the state folk dance is the square dance. Modern dance is performed by the Sanspointe Dance Company and Southern Danceworks perform in Birmingham, the Alabama Contemporary Dance Company is based in Mobile and the Alabama Repertory Dance Theatre is in Tuscaloosa.

Music enthusiasts can choose from classical to country to rock 'n' roll to jazz. The Alabama Symphony Orchestra has been around since 1921. Based in Birmingham, the orchestra also performs in Homewood. Other top orchestras are located in Huntsville, Montgomery and Gadsden. Top venues for various musical acts include Alabama Music Box (Mobile), Alabama Theatre (Birmingham), Auburn Arena, Boutwell Auditorium (Birmingham), Crossroads (Huntsville), Mobile Civic Center Arena, Montgomery Performing Arts Centre, Oak Mountain Amphitheatre (Birmingham), Saenger Theatre (Mobile), Sloss Furnace (Birmingham), Soul Kitchen (Mobile), Tuscaloosa Amphitheater, Verizon Wireless Music Center (Birmingham), Von Braun Center Concert Hall (Huntsville) and the Workplay Theatre (Birmingham).

The best opera companies are Opera Birmingham, Mobile Opera and the University of Alabama Opera.

Alabama is home to a variety of film festivals, including the Sidewalk Moving Picture Festival (Birmingham), the Birmingham International Film Festival, the Alice Film Festival (Birmingham), the Rocket Short Festival (Huntsville), the Black Film Festival (Montgomery), the Montgomery Film Festival and the South Alabama Film Festival (Mobile).

Among the best art museums in the state are: Alabama Artists Gallery in Montgomery, Alabama Rural Heritage Center in Thomaston, American Sport Art Museum and Archives in Daphne, Birmingham Museum of Art , Carnegie Visual Arts Center in Decatur, Dowling Museum and Rudd Art Center in Ozark, Fayette Art Museum, Gadsden Museum of Art, Huntsville Museum of Art , Isabel Anderson Corner Museum and Art Center in Sylacauga, Jule Collins Smith Museum of Fine Art in Auburn, Kennedy-Douglass Center for the Arts in Florence, Mary G. Hardin Center for Cultural Arts in Gadsden, Mobile Museum of Art, Montgomery Museum of Fine Art, Tuscaloosa Museum of Art and the Wiregrass Museum of Art in Dothan.

Other museums of note include Alabama Constitution Village in Huntsville (reenacting life in 1819), Alabama Department of Archives and History in Montgomery (the official state archives and museum), the Alabama Jazz Hall of Fame in Birmingham, Alabama Museum of Health Sciences in Birmingham, the Alabama Museum of Natural History in Tuscaloosa, the Alabama Music Hall of Fame in Tuscumbia, the Alabama Sports Hall of Fame in Birmingham, the Anniston Museum of Natural History, the Bessemer Hall of History, the George Washington Carver Museum in Tuskegee, the Gulf Coast Exploreum in Mobile, the McWane Science Center in Birmingham, the Mobile Carnival Museum, the National African American Archives and Museum in Mobile and the U.S. Space & Rocket Center in Huntsville.

Arts & Entertainment Crossword

Solution on page 155.

Across

1. Dreamland BBQ offering
4. Involuntary twitch
9. Kind of signal for the Cherokee tribe
14. Birmingham Zoo flightless bird
15. Use a soapbox at the Alabama Capitol
16. *Roots* writer
17. The Village at Midtown mailing abbr.
18. Alabama Women's Hall of Fame member ___ Marie Bender
19. First secretary of homeland security
20. With 59-Across, plan to get creative people teaching in Alabama schools
23. Geneva State Forest unit
24. Coast Guard rank: Abbr.
25. Magic City Grille brunch choice
28. Razzleberries cola drinker's request
30. Dine at Fife's
31. Wash. neighbor
32. Apply gently to a canvas
34. Hit on the head
35. Purge
36. May honoree
39. Ashley Furniture convertible (2 wds.)
42. "Absolutely!"
43. *Aladdin* prince
44. Neither's partner
45. Have the meatloaf at John's City Diner
47. 18-wheeler on I-65
48. "What's the ___?"
49. Recurring theme
53. Popular Mexican beer at El Camino Real restaurant
55. Quiznos sandwich, briefly
58. 1492 ship of note
59. See 20-Across (2 wds.)
62. Cantina Laredo compadre
64. Rhino relative
65. Start of an Isabella HS cheer: "Gimme ___!" (2 wds.)
66. Irishman Ditch or Mobile Channel, e.g.
67. Upright
68. Harmony Park Safari lair
69. The way things are going
70. Regions Financial executive benefits
71. Poet's palindromic preposition

Down

1. Flinches, say
2. Bring in to the Port of Mobile
3. Who often "did it" in a Random Acts whodunit
4. Scotch's partner at The Nook
5. Investigation by an Alabama Legislature committee
6. Mobile baseball stadium name
7. Mixes a drink at The Rare Martini
8. City near Phoenix
9. Bubba Gump catch
10. Bangor's state
11. Display flown in front of all Alabama post offices (2 wds.)
12. Downtown Pub beer barrel
13. Hurricane's center
21. Starring role for a Theatre Tuscaloosa show
22. Top secret?

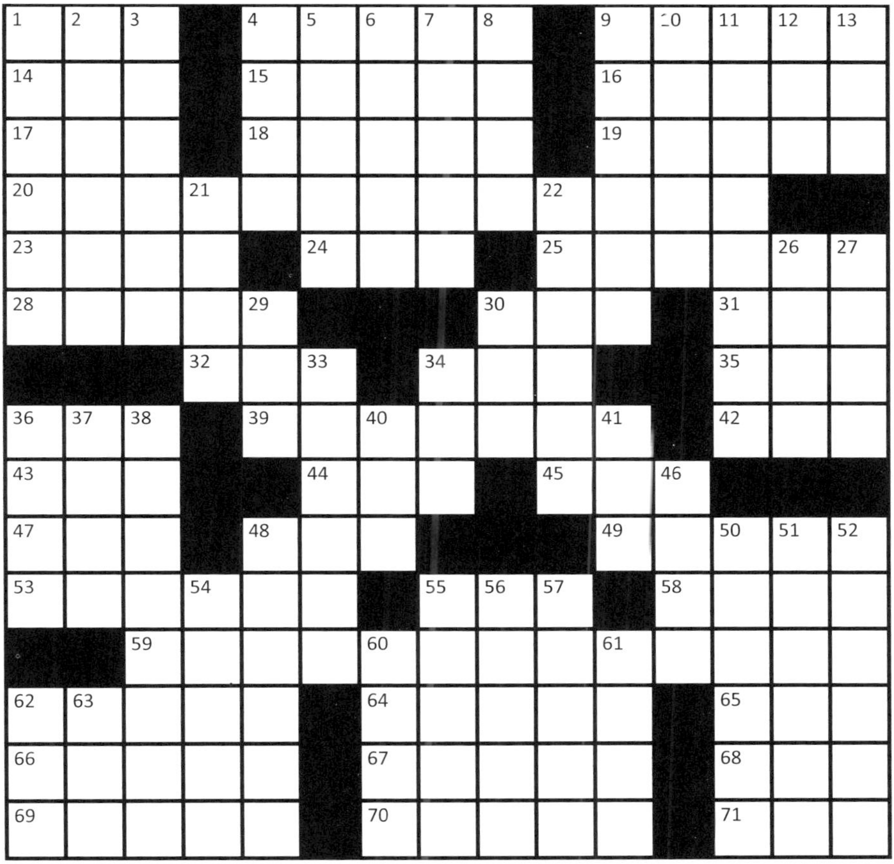

26. Second closest Great Lake to Huntsville
27. ___ Montana Grill
29. Used to be
30. Cry loudly
33. Small woody plant at Ginza Japanese Restaurant
34. Tuscaloosa tavern
36. Cleopatra's love: ___ Antony
37. Hodgepodge
38. Major headache
40. Crimson Tide opponent
41. Coosa River obstruction
46. Chinese mafia
48. Still a secret
50. Tongue-lashing
51. More nonsensical
52. A severe shortage of food
54. Trinity Episcopal Church choir accompaniment
55. Impolite look
56. UAB dorm bunk option
57. Third little pig's material
60. Beachbody Aerobics bit
61. Table scraps
62. Be in a Commedia del Arte cast
63. Fountain City Arts Festival mo.

HARDIN SUDOKU

Use logic to fill in the grid so every row, column and 2x3 box contains the letters H-A-R-D-I-N, in honor of the Mary G. Hardin Center for Cultural Arts in Gadsden. Solution on page 156.

H		A	N		R
I		R	A		
		D	R		I
R		I	D		H

PLAYHOUSE SUDOKU

Use logic to fill in the boxes so every row, column and 3x3 box contains the letters P-L-A-Y-H-O-U-S-E, in honor of the Fantasy Playhouse in Huntsville. The children's theatre began in 1961. Solution on page 156.

U		S						A
	Y		O				P	
				E				U
			Y		E		U	
		O				H		
	E		S		L			
E				L				
	P				H		S	
H						E		O

FRAMED ARTISTS

Each square contains the 8-letter name of an American artist whose work is part of the Birmingham Museum of Art collection. The name can be found by beginning at one of the letters and reading either clockwise or counterclockwise. Solution on page 156.

1.

D	**E**	**N**
N		**H**
E	**V**	**O**

2.

L	**E**	**C**
A		**N**
W	**R**	**E**

3.

E	**R**	**S**
Y		**D**
N	**O**	**L**

4.

A	**T**	**L**
E		**E**
H	**W**	**Y**

5.

D	**R**	**A**
T		**H**
G	**E**	**R**

6.

N	**B**	**R**
A		**I**
M	**G**	**D**

BUSINESS

The five largest employers in the state are (according to the *Birmingham Business Journal*):

1. Redstone Arsenal (a U.S. Army base in Huntsville with 25,373 employees)
2. University of Alabama at Birmingham
3. Maxwell Air Force Base
4. State of Alabama
5. Mobile County School Systems

The top industries in the state are aerospace, education, banking, health care, automobile manufacturing, mineral extraction, steel production and fabrication.

Alabama's Gross State Product for 2010 was $174 billion, which ranked 25th in the U.S. However, the per capita average of $36,333 ranked 46th in the nation.

The lone Alabama business on the 2012 *Fortune* 500 list of largest companies is Regions Financial Corp., at No. 343 (down from No. 293 the year before). Regions—based in Birmingham—is the holding company for Regions Bank, which operates more than 1,700 banking offices in 16 Midwest and Southern states.

Other large publically traded companies in the state are Vulcan Materials (Birmingham), HealthSouth Corp. (Birmingham), Energen Corp. (Birmingham) and Walter Energy (Birmingham).

Vulcan produces construction aggregates as well as asphalt mix, ready-mixed concrete and cement; HealthSouth operates inpatient and outpatient rehabilitation hospitals throughout the U.S.; Energen acquires, explores, develops and produces oil and natural gas; and Walter Energy produces and exports metallurgical coal for the steel industry and serves electric utility and industrial customers.

Among the largest privately held companies in the state are Drummond Co. Inc. (coal mining and processing, real estate), EBSCO Industries, Inc. (printing, information services), O'Neal Industries Inc. (metals), Brasfield & Gorrie LLC (construction), McWane Inc. (manufacturer of ductile iron pipe and other products), American Cast Iron Pipe Co. (another manufacturer of ductile iron pipe) and the Piggly Wiggly Alabama Distributing Co. Inc. (grocery distribution).

Business Alabama selects the "Best Companies to Work for in Alabama." The best large companies (250+ employees) are:

1. Baker Donelson (a law firm with offices in Birmingham and Montgomery)
2. Edward Jones
3. America's First Federal Credit Union
4. Alacare Home Health & Hospice
5. Boyd Bros Transportation, Inc.

The best medium sized companies (50-249 employees) to work for are:

1. CTS, Inc. (a regional IT consulting firm with offices in Birmingham and Mobile and other Southeastern cities)
2. MetLife Financial Group of the South
3. Legacy Community Federal Credit Union
4. White-Spunner Construction
5. Premier Bank of the South

And the best small companies (less than 50 employees) are:

1. Southern States Bank (a community bank that began in 2007 and has offices in Anniston, Opelika, Birmingham and Sylacauga)
2. ASF Logistics
3. Meyer Vacation Rentals
4. ITAC Solutions
5. Proventix Systems, Inc.

Business Crossword

Solution on page 155.

Across

1. Accompanies musically sans words
5. Jellied garnish at Bottega Restaurant
10. Deplaned at Atmore Municipal Airport
14. UA term paper footnote abbr.
15. Silver Stirrup Stables enclosure
16. Anatomical knot at Providence Hospital
17. It's a long story
18. Electronics pioneer Nikola
19. Huntsville Fencing Club battle
20. Athletic equipment company based in Birmingham (2 wds.)
23. Alabama State University map blurb: "You ___ here"
24. Good name for a Bama lawyer?
25. True-blue, like a Crimson Tide fan
29. Poetic tribute
32. To-do list
36. Disinclined
38. Suffix with ideal
40. House of Martial Arts discipline: ___ Chi
41. Producer of construction stone, sand and gravel with headquarters in Birmingham (2 wds.)
45. Regions Center building wing
46. Pester for payment
47. Dothan Country Club sand trap clubs
48. Hem again at Mo's Alterations
51. Semmes Azalea Festival mo.
53. Domineering in a Confederate Motors boardroom
54. Unruly head of hair
56. "Act your ___!"
58. Birmingham company with lots of reading material
65. Opelika Farmers Market veggie
66. Get out of a Comfort Inn bed
67. Jordan-Hare Stadium section
69. Energen Corporation number two, informally
70. Stalin's predecessor
71. Distinctive flair
72. Knock off a dragon
73. Selma Water Works conduits
74. ___ *Breckinridge*

Down

1. "For ___ a jolly . . . "
2. The Beehive State
3. Three wise men in a First Baptist Church creche
4. Generous slice of the coconut pie at Gibson's Bar-B-Q
5. Fall flower at A Bloom Garden Center
6. Passe UAB dorm room staple
7. Time gone by
8. Misfortunes
9. Applauds a good play by the Tigers
10. Mitchell of WVTM-TV's network news
11. Boor
12. Fateful day for Caesar
13. Diversified Resources business card abbr.
21. Hobby Lobby model wood
22. Regions Park ump's call
25. Two-time U.S. Open tennis champ
26. Rudimentary seed
27. Screams for the UA volley team at Foster Auditorium
28. Circle segment in a Curry HS math class
30. *American Idol* contestant DeGarmo from Birmingham
31. Phenix City winter hrs.

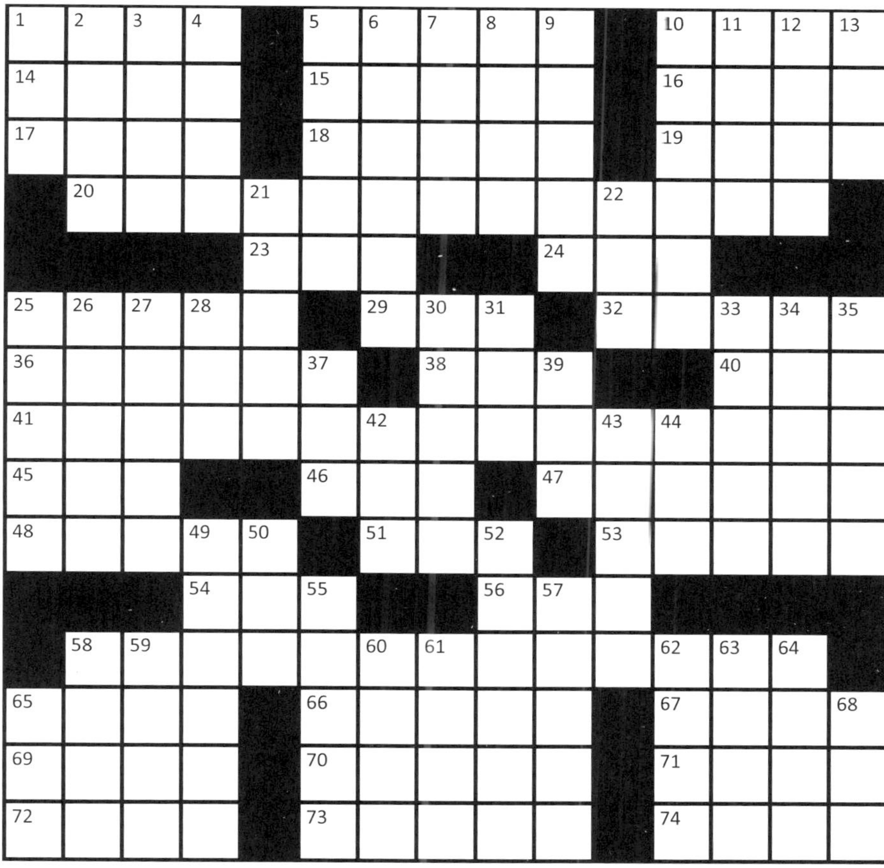

33. Bucks at Tatum Creek Hunting Camp
34. Winn-Dixie greens
35. Hardly a he-man
37. Brookwood HS lineman
39. Kitten's cry at PetSmart
42. Ornamental bloom at Albert's Flowers
43. Alabama soldier in the Civil War
44. Wedding vow (2 wds.)
49. PayPal cash
50. Chef Sake's Restaurant pan
52. Kind of Panera fruit bread
55. Second Baptist Church sacred hymn
57. Secluded valleys
58. Faulkner State culinary class recipe direction
59. Black-and-white predator
60. Alabama atlas stat
61. Short skirt at The Limited
62. Big-ticket ___
63. Greasy at Jiffy Lube
64. Close by, like Georgia
65. Walgreens competitor
68. Genetics letters

Boeing Sudoku

Use logic to fill in the grid so every row, column and 2x3 box contains the letters B-O-E-I-N-G, in honor of the aerospace company with facilities in Huntsville. Solution on page 156.

	I	G			
		N	B		
		I	N		B
O		B	I		
		O	E		
			G	I	

Brasfield Sudoku

Use the letters B-R-A-S-F-I-E-L-D (in honor of Brasfield & Gorrie General Contractors with corporate headquarters in Birmingham) and use logic to fill in the grid so that every row and column contains those letters. Not all the nine-letter "boxes" are square—they're shifted—but the solving rules remain the same. Solution on page 156.

				S	B			
				L		R		B
I	D						A	
		R	E			D		
			D			I		E
			A		L			
	F	D						
L								I
		A		R			S	

CROSSWORD CONSTRUCTOR

It's your turn to be a crossword puzzle constructor. Using the New York Stock Exchange symbol PRA (for ProAssurance Corporation which is based in Birmingham) in the diagonal, complete the grid with three three-letter words (or names or abbreviations commonly found in crossword puzzles) going across that also make three three-letter words (or names or abbreviations) going down. There are several possible solutions. Ours is on page 157. HINT: The letters we used to complete the puzzle are under the grid.

<table>
<tr><td>P</td><td></td><td></td></tr>
<tr><td></td><td>R</td><td></td></tr>
<tr><td></td><td></td><td>A</td></tr>
</table>

E E E I P R

Now try another one. Using the NYSE symbol CLP (for Colonial Properties Trust which has its headquarters in Birmingham) in the diagonal, complete the grid with three three-letter words (or names or abbreviations commonly found in crossword puzzles) going across that also make three three-letter words (or names or abbreviations) going down. Our solution on page 157. HINT: The letters we used to complete the puzzle are under the grid.

<table>
<tr><td>C</td><td></td><td></td></tr>
<tr><td></td><td>L</td><td></td></tr>
<tr><td></td><td></td><td>P</td></tr>
</table>

A A A E R T

Education

The Alabama State Board of Education oversees the 67 county school boards and 60 city boards of education. There are 1,541 schools that provide education for nearly 750,000 elementary and secondary school students. A recent ranking of states' education systems put Alabama at No. 47 in how high school students performed in math and science (ahead of just Louisiana, West Virginia and Mississippi).

The Alabama Commission on Higher Education oversees 14 four-year public universities and two-year community colleges and 17 private undergraduate and graduate universities.

The largest college in the state is The University of Alabama at Tuscaloosa (30,127 students), followed by Troy University (28,322), Auburn University (25,078), the University of Alabama at Birmingham (17,543) and the University of South Alabama (14,776).

The University of Alabama was founded in 1831 and offers programs of study in 13 academic divisions. There are nearly 300 buildings on the 1,970-acre campus. The center of campus is the Quad, which features the Gorgas Library on the north end and the Denny Chimes on the south. Included on campus are the Alabama Museum of Natural History, the Paul W. Bryant Museum and the UA Arboretum.

Troy University was founded in 1887. In addition to the main campus in Troy, the school has branches in Montgomery, Phenix City and Dothan. Troy is renowned for its programs and services to traditional, nontraditional and military students, as well as its online academic programs. Troy was ranked by the Institute of International Education as the 25th best university in the U.S. for international students.

Auburn University was established in 1856 as the East Alabama Male College. It has grown to become one of only a few universities designated as a land-grant, sea-grant and space-grant research center. It has been ranked among the top 50 public schools by *U.S. News & World Report* for 19 consecutive years. Traditions include "Callouts" on the steps of Cater Hall for new members of organizations, "Hey Day" which promotes friendliness on campus and "Ask Foy," a telephone and walk-in information service in the Student Union.

The University of Alabama at Birmingham began in 1936 and became an autonomous institution in 1969. It offers more than 140 programs in 12 academic divisions and is known for its medical research and natural sciences programs. The campus is divided into three sections: the Medical District, the Academic Center and Athletics Facilities. At the center of the school is the Campus Green.

The University of South Alabama is located in Mobile and was established in 1964. USA is divided into 10 colleges and offers more than 50 bachelor's degrees and more than 40 master's degree programs. The student-faculty ratio is 22:1 with 41.5 percent of the classes having fewer than 20 students.

Other leading universities include Tuskegee University, Alabama A&M (Normal), Samford University (Birmingham), Alabama State (Montgomery), Jacksonville State, University of North Alabama (Florence), Spring Hill College (Mobile), University of Alabama in Huntsville, University of Mobile, University of Montevallo and University of West Alabama (Livingston).

The smallest school is Heritage Christian University with 88 students; the largest two-year college is Calhoun Community College in Decatur (12,000+ students). The oldest schools are the University of North Alabama and Spring Hill College, both established in 1830.

There are two medical schools in the state (UAB and South Alabama) and five law schools (UA, Samford, Faulkner, Birmingham and Miles).

Education Crossword

Solution on page 157.

Across

1. Carrabba's Italian Grill wine choice: ___ Grigio
6. Hurricane Ivan wind
10. Burn slightly at Ruth's Chris
14. Mix-up
15. Black cat, maybe
16. Suffer from
17. UA football figures
18. Iridescent gem at Zales
19. On the safe side, in the Gulf
20. Birmingham Zoo elephant's weight, maybe
21. Youngster at Rock Quarry Elementary School
23. Baptist university located at Homewood
25. Young Alabama socialites
26. Kendrick Gourmet Food caviar
27. Cheek coloring
29. Multi-state lottery game: ___ Millions
31. Athens City School District org.
34. Whirlpool or tornado
35. Eur. land
36. Snob
37. With speed
38. Beef 'O' Brady's brew
39. Slick goo
40. Like Huntingdon Coll. founders
41. Mine find
42. Pieces for piano class
43. Opposite of post-
44. Male turkeys at the Alabama State Fair
45. Points at a Stix Restaurant table
46. Bama barn hooter
47. Be ill-humored
48. Huntsville school operated by the Seventh-day Adventist Church
52. Common Dads Club soccer game score
53. "___ show time!"
56. Huntsville Bible College prayer ending
57. Astronomer's sighting at the Kiesel Park Observatory
59. Big picture at the Alabama State Capitol
61. Fine-tune
62. Unappetizing school cafeteria serving
63. Flaming
64. Cold war inits.
65. Puts in stitches in a Home Ec class
66. Barely beat at Mobile Greyhound Park

Down

1. Attention-getting sound at the Auburn University Libraries
2. "What's gotten ___ you?"
3. Bombay Grill bread
4. Poetic adverb
5. Macon County school that is a National Historic Landmark
6. Merchandise
7. Lake Martin Amphitheatre equipment
8. Meadows
9. Blow up at One Hour Photo
10. Rub raw
11. Head light?
12. Allege as fact in Greene County Court
13. Kind of ASO instrument
22. Wild mountain goat
24. Extinct kin of the kiwi
25. Like Rembrandt or Van Gogh
27. Cowboy, at times
28. Use a soapbox at the Jefferson County Courthouse
29. Fairfield college that features the Purple Marching Machine

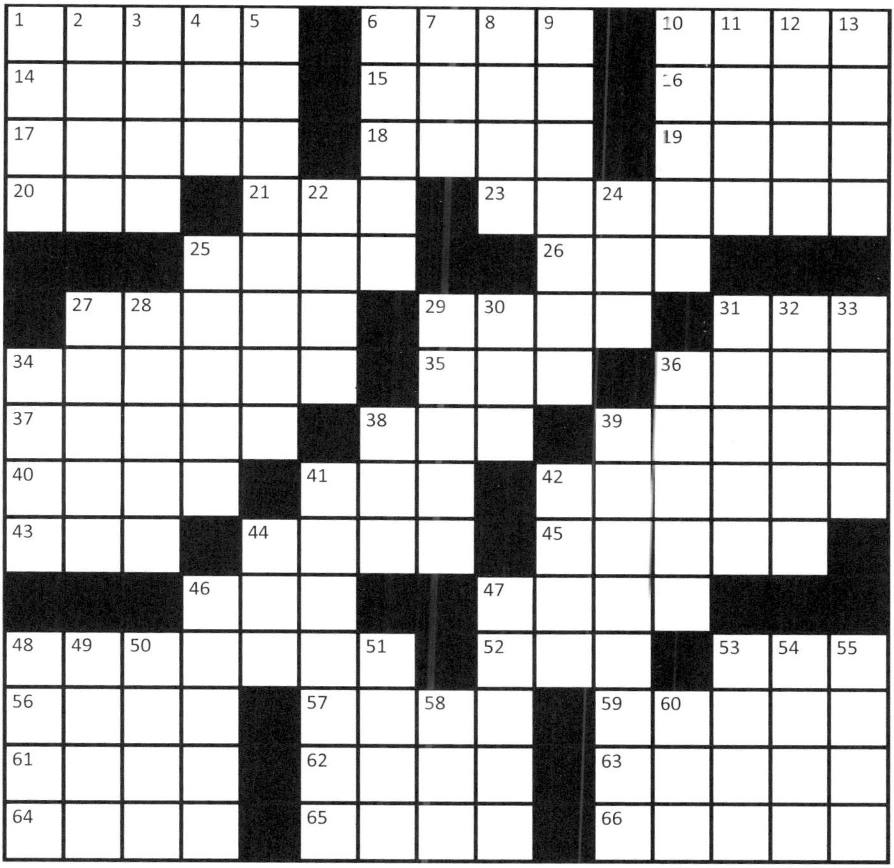

30. "Able was I ___ . . ."
31. A deadly sin
32. Fort Payne ___-*Journal*
33. Matures, like a wine at Ozan Vineyard
34. Seductress
36. Put (down), as money
38. Foley HS quarterback's asset
39. Historically black liberal arts college at West Tuscaloosa
41. Sarabella Cafe & Tea Room varieties
42. Needle case
44. Tango requirement for the Crimson Tide Ballroom Dancers
46. Dog tag datum
47. Ginger cookies at Kroger
48. Hawaiian island
49. Old Testament book
50. Some male dolls at Toys"R"Us
51. Winner in Alabama in the 1996 U.S. Presidential election
53. Tennessee's state flower
54. Container weight
55. Winter transport
58. Solemn promise
60. ET's craft

COLLEGES WORD SEARCH

Solution on page 157.

L	Y	M	H	F	F	S	A	M	F	O	R	D	N	M
X	O	E	U	O	A	K	W	O	O	D	D	L	D	O
S	R	T	N	E	U	A	I	N	I	G	R	I	V	B
E	T	A	T	S	L	L	I	V	E	B	E	M	V	I
L	S	T	I	E	K	A	X	F	T	T	I	M	Y	L
I	P	S	N	T	N	B	T	S	A	A	D	O	T	E
M	R	P	G	A	E	A	U	T	T	L	S	N	N	F
S	I	O	D	T	R	M	S	I	S	L	T	T	O	G
E	N	H	O	S	A	A	K	L	S	A	A	E	S	D
G	G	S	N	D	M	A	E	L	N	D	T	V	D	A
D	H	I	N	A	L	&	G	M	E	E	E	A	U	U
I	I	B	B	E	E	M	E	A	H	G	S	L	J	B
R	L	A	Y	N	S	O	E	N	T	A	K	L	Q	U
M	L	A	W	S	O	N	S	T	A	T	E	O	V	R
A	I	D	R	O	C	N	O	C	A	L	H	O	U	N

ALABAMA A&M
ALABAMA STATE
AMRIDGE
ATHENS STATE
AUBURN
BEVILL STATE
BISHOP STATE
CALHOUN
CONCORDIA
FAULKNER
HUNTINGDON
JUDSON
LAWSON STATE
MILES
MOBILE
MONTEVALLO
OAKWOOD
REID STATE
SAMFORD
SELMA
SNEAD STATE
SPRING HILL
STILLMAN
TALLADEGA
TROY
TUSKEGEE
VIRGINIA

Where are They?

Match each of these Alabama colleges with the town where its main campus is located. Solution on page 157.

1. Alabama State University
2. Concordia College
3. Judson College
4. Miles College
5. Oakwood University
6. Samford University
7. Stillman College
8. University of North Alabama
9. University of South Alabama
10. University of West Alabama

a. Birmingham
b. Fairfield
c. Florence
d. Huntsville
e. Livingston
f. Marion
g. Mobile
h. Montgomery
i. Selma
j. Tuscaloosa

History

Long before Alabama came into existence, the region was occupied by indigenous peoples of various cultures. European explorers arrived in 1528 and settlers followed in 1663. The English were the first to lay claim on the area, followed by the French.

The English gained undisputed control in 1763 with the Treaty of Paris, which ended the French and Indian War. During the American Revolutionary War, the British ceded the area to Spain. In 1795 when the Treaty of Madrid was signed, Spain ceded the land to the U.S.

However, Native Americans still occupied much of the region. U.S. forces, led by Gen Andrew Jackson, pushed back the Native Americans and Alabama was admitted as the 22nd state in 1819.

The state's economy was driven by large cotton plantations worked by African slaves. By 1860, there were 435,000 enslaved workers, which represented about 45 percent of the state's population.

When the Union sought to abolish slavery, Alabama joined forces with other Southern states and seceded from the Union in 1861. More than 35,000 Alabamans died in the Civil War; another 30,000 were seriously disabled. With the end of slavery, the cotton plantations suffered.

Cotton plantations didn't disappear entirely, but the new Alabama economy was heavy industry and mining. By 1915, 25 percent of the nation's iron was produced in Alabama.

African-Americans and whites remained segregated. White state legislatures attempted to prevent advancement by the African-Americans. When the legislature couldn't hold back the Civil Rights Movement, the Ku Klux Klan stepped in with intimidation and violence.

Led by Rev. Martin Luther King, Jr., the Civil Rights Movement gained a foothold nationwide. Alabama eventually accepted desegregation and equality. The state's political leadership shifted from the Democratic Party to the Republican Party.

During that time, Alabama's economy again made a transition, moving to technology and the expansion of military installations. Huntsville became the center of the nation's research in space exploration. Birmingham became the state's business leader. Mobile was the gateway to the Gulf. And Montgomery continued as the backbone of state government.

Today, Alabama is the 30th largest state with 52,419 square miles and the 23rd most populous state with 4.8 million residents.

As for the future, Gov. Robert Bentley quoted from the Bible: "Brothers, count it all joy when trials come into your life." Added Bentley, "What it's talking about is when we have difficulties in our lives, it makes us stronger. And so we ought to be thankful."

Official Alabama Symbols

SONG:
"Alabama"

FLOWER:
Camellia

BIRD:
Yellowhammer

GAME BIRD:
Wild Turkey

ANIMAL:
Black Bear

SALTWATER FISH:
Atlantic tarpon

FRESHWATER FISH:
Largemouth bass

HORSE:
Racking horse

NUT:
Pecan

INSECT:
Monarch butterfly

REPTILE:
Alabama red-bellied turtle

GEMSTONE:
Star Blue Quartz

MINERAL:
Hematite

ROCK:
Marble

MASCOT AND BUTTERFLY:
Eastern Tiger Swallowtail

TREE:
Southern Longleaf Pine

WILDFLOWER:
Oak-leaf hydrangea

FRUIT:
Blackberry

TREE FRUIT:
Peach

History Crossword

Solution on page 158.

Across

1. Trudge
5. Alabama flag color
10. Performance at Alys Robinson Stephens Performing Arts Center
14. Like a WTVY newscast
15. Overhangs on a Philip Woods home
16. Wander Alabama
17. Face-to-face exam at Troy University
18. Pelham-born guitarist Hinds
19. Bear Bryant, e.g.
20. Alabama governor who called for " . . . segregation now, segregation tomorrow, segregation forever"
22. First Alabama governor following the Civil War
24. Pillow cover at Bed Bath & Beyond
25. *Birmingham News* bit
26. Select, with "for"
29. The middle of summer?
30. Indian Springs School volleyball court divider
31. Fan setting
34. Allegation in Barbour County Court
36. One of two certainties
38. Continental currency
39. Remote button
40. Make reparations
42. More reliable
43. Common Commandment word
44. Black Warrior River obstruction
47. Morning moisture at Big Spring Park
49. "___ we there yet?"
50. Fong's Alterations concern
51. Distinctive flair
53. Native American people who occupied the territory that became Alabama
56. Official state insect that is a colorful butterfly
60. Tibetan priest
61. Started a cigarette (2 wds.)
63. Send to the canvas in an Alabama Golden Gloves fight
64. Eurasia's ___ Mountains
65. Habituate
66. UAB term paper footnote abbr.
67. Dixie Overland Highway curve
68. Moorehead of *Bewitched*
69. Say it ain't so

Down

1. Newman's Farm Supply purchase
2. Old Italian bread?
3. White House office shape
4. Vales
5. Internet video device
6. Sheiks' cliques
7. Cole Porter song: "___ Got You Under My Skin"
8. What might be left standing at Vestavia Bowl (2 wds.)
9. Plantation with a groundskeeper, maybe
10. Light refractor
11. Wacky
12. Houston County town that shares its name with an English river
13. Urges

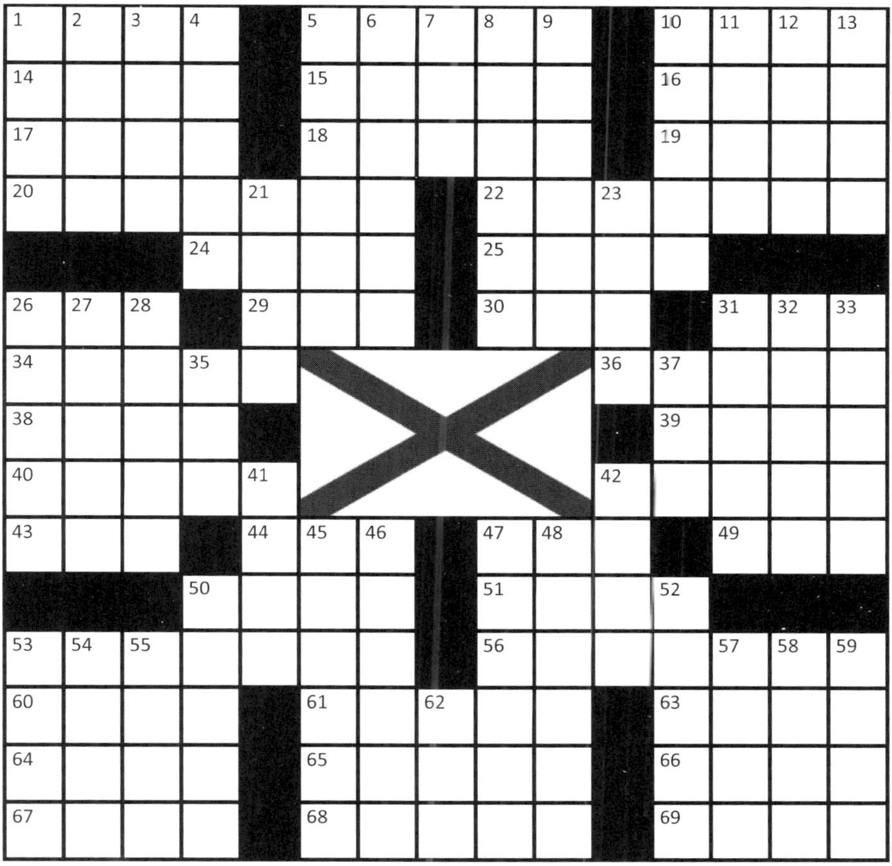

21. "Uh . . . excuse me"
23. Abbr. after many a general's name
26. Atlantic or Pacific
27. Disney dog
28. Fortuneteller's card
31. First lady after Hillary
32. Cahaba River romper
33. One of the five Ws for an *Anniston Star* reporter
35. Charged particle
37. Cousin of an ostrich
41. Blue-pencil an article in *Alabama Living*
42. Alabama Ballet performance: "___ Lake"
45. Spring bloomer
46. Kitten's crying at the Sumter County Humane Society shelter
47. Shy
48. Acts on a sudden itching for a hitching
50. Burn with hot water
52. Like an Auburn streaker
53. Listing in a Sweet Water HS yearbook
54. Tortoise racer
55. Muscat's land
57. PNC Bank posting
58. Shade of blue at Kinko's
59. Sacred
62. Morgan Creek Vineyards cask

Alabama Time Line

Match each of these events with the year in which it occurred. Solution on page 157.

1. Alabama became a state
2. Alabama joined the Confederate States of America
3. Guy Hunt elected governor
4. Hank Aaron was born in Mobile
5. Montgomery selected as the state capital
6. Birmingham airport opened
7. Gen. Andrew Jackson defeated the Creek Indians
8. "Heart of Dixie" slogan first used on license plates
9. Birmingham founded
10. Hurricane Frederick hit the Gulf Coast

a. 1814
b. 1819
c. 1846
d. 1861
e. 1871
f. 1931
g. 1934
h. 1955
i. 1979
j. 1986

ALABAMA CITIES FROM A TO Z

Complete the names of these Alabama cities by filling in the blanks with the letters provided. Solution on page 157.

A __ __ A	LM
B __ B B __ __	AEI
C __ C __ __	EIL
D __ __ __ __ __ D	AIMNO
E __ __ __ __ E	LMOR
F __ F F __	EY
G __ __ G __ __	EEIR
H __ __ __ H	AET
I __ __ I __ __ __ __ __	GNNORTV
J __ __ __ __	AOPP
K __ __ K	IR
L __ L L __ __ __	AIIN
M __ M __ __ __ __	EHIPS
N __ __ __ __ N	EOTW
O __ __ O __	INR
P __ __ __ P __ __ __	CEORST
Q __ __ __ __ __ __	INNOTU
R __ __ __ R	AEM
S __ __ __ S	AIL
T __ T __ __	ISU
U __ __ __ __	INTY
V __ __ __ __ V __ __	ADEINR
W __ __ __ __ W	AARS
__ X __ __ __	CEEL
Y __ __ __ __ __ Y	AELNT
Z __ __ __ __ __ __	CIIPTY

Recreation

There are 24 state parks in Alabama providing plenty of venues for boating, camping, fishing, hiking, biking, waterskiing, hunting and almost anything else you want to do.

One can even explore a ghost town. Historic Blakeley State Park in Baldwin County is the site of a major fort during the Civil War. It is also listed on the National Register of Historic Places.

Or soak in a mineral springs bath. Bladon Springs State Park in Choctaw County is centered around four springs. Many visitors bathe in the water that is also potable.

Or explore caves. Cathedral Caverns State Park in Marshall County is a National Natural Landmark. The cave's entrance is 25 feet tall by 128 feet wide, making it the widest entrance of any commercial cave in the world. A single column inside is 45 feet tall and 243 feet in circumference, making it the largest column in the world. The largest room is 792 feet long and 200 feet wide.

The oldest continuously operating state park is Cheaha. Located in Clay and Cleburne counties, the 2,799-acre park is home to a lodge, restaurant, general store, campground and hiking trails.

There are four national forests in Alabama: the William B. Bankhead National Forest covering 181,230 acres and known as the "land of a thousand waterfalls;" the Talladega National Forest covering 392,567 acres on the southern edge of the Appalachian Mountains; Tuskegee National Forest covering 11,252 acres; and Conecuh National Forest covering 83,000 acres.

For fishermen, there are plenty of great lakes. The largest is Lake Guntersville with a surface area of 69,100 acres, followed by Wheeler Lake (68,300) near Decatur, Eufaula Lake (45,180) and Pickwick Lake (41,515) near Florence.

ROBERT TRENT JONES GOLF TRAIL

The Robert Trent Jones Golf Trail began as an investment for the Retirement Systems of Alabama (RSA). Dr. David Bronner, CEO of the organization conceived of the idea to effectively diversify the assets of the state's pension fund while helping the state's economy. "The stronger the Retirement Systems of Alabama can make Alabama, the stronger the Retirement Systems will be," he said. "I don't do windows, and I don't do just 18s."

Today, the Trail is comprised of 468 holes on 26 courses at 11 sites stretching across the entire state: from Dothan to Florence and from Mobile to Huntsville. All the courses reflect the design philosophy of legendary golf course architect Robert Trent Jones, Sr. (an Englishman who moved to the U.S. at a young age and is credited with designing more than 500 golf courses worldwide).

Several of the courses are part of larger resorts that include hotels, spas and other amenities. Two of the courses are home to professional events: the Navistar LPGA Classic at Capitol Hill (Prattville) and the Mobile Bay LPGA Classic at Magnolia Grove (Mobile).

The Trail opened in 1992 with four courses (in Opelika, Huntsville, Mobile and Birmingham). Three courses were added the following year (in Dothan, Greenville and Anniston). Four additional courses were added later (in Prattville, Hoover, Point Clear and Florence).

As an investment, the RSA admits that the Trail is only marginally profitable, but the construction and tourism dollars that it helped create have been valued at more than a billion dollars.

The courses were designed, and continue to be set up, to be playable by golfers of all ages and abilities. The same course can be played from 4,700 yards to 7,700 yards.

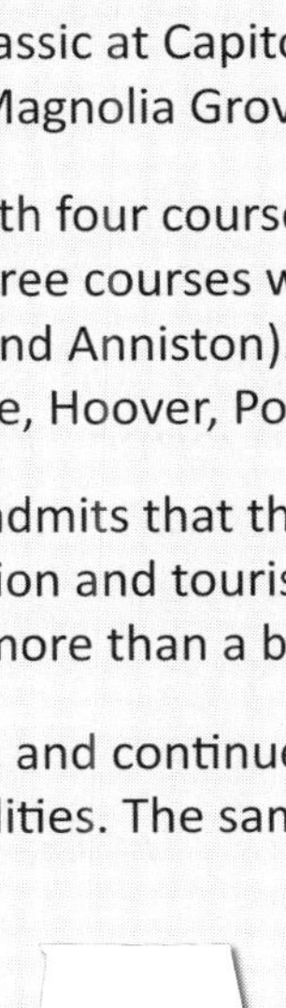

Recreation Crossword

Solution on page 158.

Across

1. Like a few Jenny Craig clients
6. Roulette bet at Riverside Casino
9. One of the Jackson 5
13. Wikipedia co-founder who was born in Huntsville
14. Piece of Crimson Tide football gear
15. Alabama Highway Patrol helicopter part
16. State Park located on the banks of Lake Eufaula
18. Money in North Alabama Bank, say
19. Inebriated
20. Rite Aid competitor
21. Wintzell's Oyster House kitchen meas.
24. Fury
25. Auburn fraternity letter
26. 320 Salon, e.g.
29. Card game
31. Its ingredient list starts with sugar and ends with chocolate
32. Port of Mobile craft
33. Knit Stop supply
34. Genuflect at St. Maurice Parish
35. UN workers' grp. that won a Nobel Peace Prize
36. Choctaw County State Park that was originally a health resort (2 wds.)
40. Robertsdale HS science class, briefly
41. S-shaped moldings
42. Islamic Society of Tuscaloosa leader
44. Park in Montevallo that features tree carvings
45. Sitter's headache
46. Empathize
48. *Sand Mountain Reporter* revenue source
49. Madison Hospital unit
50. Southwood Presbyterian Church minister: Abbr.
51. Marbury HS volleyball match part
52. U.S. soldiers
53. Time of hysteria
55. Start
58. Largest state-owned park in the U.S. (2 wds.)
62. Toots one's own horn
63. Mail Boxes ___
64. Klingler's Black Forest dessert
65. Untrustworthy types
66. Scrooge's cry
67. Desoto Falls effect

Down

1. Hooter's symbol
2. Alabama State Fair barn sound
3. Lodge #393 member
4. Bit of watermelon waste
5. ___ de corps
6. Share one's views
7. Dungeonlike
8. Banned pesticide
9. Joe Namath's light throw
10. Part of TGIF
11. Finish Line shoe part
12. Food scrap
15. Romano's Macaroni Grill entree
17. Willa Cather's *One of* ___
20. Yell for the Tigers
21. Commandment pronoun
22. Petrel or gull, e.g.

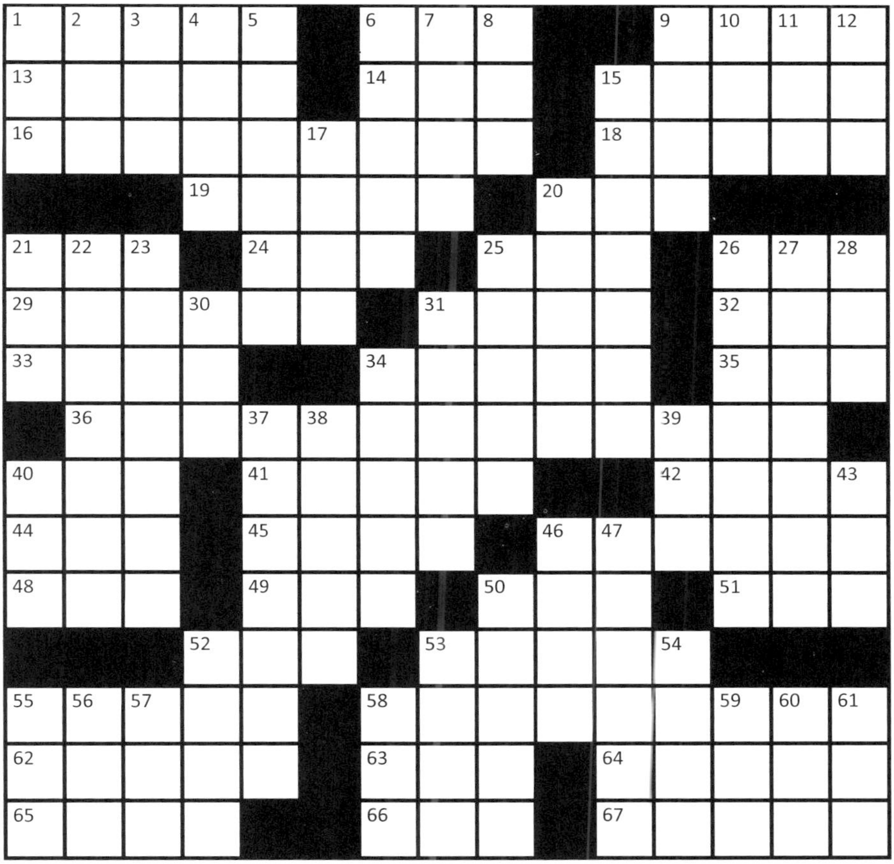

23. Places for pizza or ice cream
25. Warms up
26. Marks of shame
27. Throb, like the music at Rhythm and Brews
28. "Give it ___!" (2 wds.)
30. Genetic inits.
31. Get-go
34. Work, as dough, at Bunny Bread Co.
37. Plodding workhorses in children's stories
38. Fairy tale baddies
39. Zilch
40. Birmingham Zoo constrictor
43. Bumped into at Village Mall
46. Tear to pieces
47. Ousts from Gazebo Apartments
50. Zazu Gastropub dressing choice
52. Commodores band jobs
53. Fast food sandwich restaurant: ___ Pit
54. Cotton or corn
55. English channel
56. Birmingham Barons pitcher's stat
57. Wander aimlessly
58. Part of www
59. Be human
60. Montgomery Regional Airport posting
61. Lock opener

State Parks Word Search

Solution on page 158.

Z
W B Y
N I C E U
Q O N R L O O
H A S D Z E C U V
K C I K H
E C R S A A A
L J A E G L T R E
H A Q J E N B T O N M
P K K I Y A L
G C N E R V H A N
Q Z H A V P X O N I H
S G N I R P S N O D A L B
A C F E E E C C T
A L K C O U E H O N S
P L C A H N L L E O U W Q
N U A A S E A B R E P O Y Z Y
R W A A S D U C E M S
J O E W H E E L E R K I M
Z B L H W A T S E A X A U S H
G U L F C C Q N O K H K O P B G K
O T A
M O L
U R X

BLADON SPRINGS
BLAKELEY
BLUE SPRINGS
CHATTAHOOCHEE
CHEAHA
CHEWACLA
CHICKASAW
DESOTO
FLORALA
FRANK JACKSON
GULF
JOE WHEELER
LAKE LURLEEN
MEAHER
MONTE SANO
OAK MOUNTAIN
ROLAND COOPER
WIND CREEK

ACROSS & DOWN WORDS

There are 10 activities and a place name hidden in the grid. Taking one letter from each box across the top row, find a 4-letter activity that can be done in an Alabama State Park. Cross off the letters as you use them. Do the same for the other five rows. Then move to the first column and find a 6-letter park activity going down and cross off those letters. Do the same for the other three columns. The remaining letters, one per box, will reveal the place, reading left to right, row by row. Solution on page 159.

H L S	A J W	I K M	E M P
C I P	A E O	I M U	I N P
K S T	A R T	E I S	C L S
G I O	O R S	E L T	F N S
F N T	A I K	S T U	E H I
G H P	A I U	M N R	C K T

Across

Down

Place

Sports

Football may be king of spectator sports in Alabama, but it isn't the only athletic activity that captures the interest and spirit of the loyal fans throughout the state.

If University of Alabama and Auburn University football rank as 1 and 1a, then the spring practices of both schools likely rank 2 and 2a.

The two schools first met on the gridiron in 1893. Now the annual game—dubbed the "Iron Bowl"—is considered one of the best rivalries in all of sports. Alabama leads the series, 41 wins to 34. (There was one tie.) The game is traditionally played on Thanksgiving weekend. The game was played at the neutral site of Legion Field in Birmingham 47 times. Twice both schools entered the game undefeated. In 1971, 10-0 Alabama beat 9-0 Auburn, 31-7; and in 1994, 10-0 Alabama beat 9-0-1 Auburn, 21-14.

UA has won or shared 14 national championships (the last in 2011) and has had one Heisman Trophy winner (Mark Ingram in 2009). Auburn has won two national titles (the last in 2010) and has had three Heisman Trophy winners (Pat Sullivan in 1971, Bo Jackson in 1985 and Cam Newton in 2010).

As a testament to Alabama loving its football, Birmingham has had at least eight teams in upstart men's pro football leagues: the Birmingham Americans and Birmingham Vulcans in the World Football League (1974-75), the Alabama Vulcans in the American Football Association (1979), the Birmingham Stallions in the United States Football League (1983-85), the Birmingham Fire in the World League of American Football (1991-92), the Birmingham Barracudas in the Canadian Football League (1995), the Birmingham/Alabama Steeldogs in the af2 (2000-07) and the Birmingham Thunderbolts in the XFL (2001).

Alabama is also rabid about auto racing, specifically NASCAR. The Talladega Superspeedway is the host track for two Sprint Cup Series races: the Aaron's 499 in May and the Good Sam Roadside Assistance 500 in October. The track is also the site of NASCAR's Nationwide Series and Camping World Truck Series events. The Barber Motorsports Park in Birmingham, the Montgomery Motorsports Park and the Huntsville Dragway hold major races as well.

Alabama is the second most populous state without a major professional sports league franchise (behind Virginia). But the state is home to several professional sports teams in a variety of other sports.

There are minor league baseball teams in Birmingham, Huntsville, Mobile and Montgomery. Huntsville has an arena football team in the Professional Indoor Football League, a minor league hockey team in the Southern Professional Hockey League, a soccer team in the National Premier Soccer League (that plays in suburban Madison), a women's football team in the Independent Women's Football League and a roller derby team in the Women's Flat Track Derby Association. Birmingham also fields a team in the women's roller derby league and a minor league basketball team in the Continental Basketball League. Mobile has a basketball team in the American Basketball Association.

The Alabama High School Athletic Association offers state championships for boys in 11 sports and for girls in 11 sports. Founded in 1921, the Association oversees athletics at 401 senior high members and 287 junior high and middle school members. More than 75,000 students participate in programs annually. Its mission statement reads, in part: "Major aims of the AHSAA are to serve the needs of its member schools in conducting their interscholastic athletic programs and to assist member schools in reaching the educational objectives as established by their school systems."

Sports Crossword

Solution on page 158.

Across

1. University shopping center
5. Firm
10. Mid-State Asphalt goo
13. CVS hand lotion ingredient
14. Valuable find
15. Speed along I-65
16. Southern League team that plays in Hank Aaron Stadium (2 wds.)
19. Had the Hot Lips & Grits at Baumhower's Wings
20. Redbox rental: ___ *Brockovich*
21. Family reunion attendee
23. Penny
24. Millbrook Farmers Market sweet potato
26. Same old, same old
27. South Alabama Theatre Company cast
30. Birmingham native who became the U.S. Secretary of State
31. Yellow, Red or Black, e.g.
32. Montgomery Zoo primates
33. Itty-bitty
35. Southern Professional Hockey League team that won a championship in 2010 (2 wds.)
41. Appropriate
42. Nino's Italian Restaurant good-bye
43. "___ about time!"
46. Boxing prize
47. Oak Mountain Amphitheatre concert souvenir, often
49. Big bird of myth
50. "What's the ___?"
51. Chuck E. Cheese's pinball no-no
52. More than dislike
54. Abominable Snowman
55. West Alabama Animal Clinic doc
58. Professional Indoor Football League team that plays in the Von Braun Center (2 wds.)
62. Acquire
63. Sophia of *Two Women*
64. Opera Birmingham highlight
65. Governor Bentley photo ___ (media events)
66. Rich veins
67. Hair Reflections beautician, at times

Down

1. Baby's first word, maybe
2. "Thanks ___!" (2 wds.)
3. Earring site
4. Hula dancer's necklace
5. Backs of boats on Lake Martin
6. Elliptical path at the UNA Observatory
7. UAB student aid
8. Tuskegee University building flora
9. Cotillion girl
10. Teak House cuisine
11. Broadcasters
12. Dothan firefighter's feat
17. Sinister look
18. Catch, as in a net
22. Auburn University sorority letter
23. Walmart receipt listings
24. Triangular traffic sign
25. Keith Middle-High School breakout

27. Ooh and ___
28. PC "brain"
29. Mark of perfection for a UA gymnast
30. Rent again
33. Albertville Public Library listing
34. Gulf Shores marina sight
36. Hoover or Bessemer, e.g.
37. Competes
38. III + IV
39. Auburn Rowing Club need
40. Fort Rucker bed
43. PeoplesSouth Bank offering, for short
44. Trinidad's partner
45. Lug
47. Tennessee football team
48. Big loser's nickname?
51. Little laugh
53. 3 H Stables feedbag contents
54. Berry HS football field division
55. Part of VIP
56. Cleveland's lake
57. Old Russian autocrat
59. Apiece, in Crimson Tide scores
60. Working Cows Dairy sound
61. "Spy vs. Spy" magazine

WHAT IS IT?

These diagrams represent eight terms used in describing Alabama sports. What are they? Solution on page 159.

Football Terms

1. F
I
R
S
T

2. pas

Baseball Terms

3. league

4. **POP**

Basketball Terms

5. POINTERS
pointers
Pointers

6. DRIBBLE
DRIBBLE

Hockey Terms

7. blue |

8. **AW AY**

Mascot Match

Match each of these 19 Alabama Community College Conference schools with their team's nickname/mascot. Solution on page 159.

1. Alabama Southern	a. Bison
2. Bishop State	b. Boll Weevils
3. Calhoun	c. Buccaneers
4. Central Alabama	d. Cardinals
5. Chattahoochee Valley	e. Cougars
6. Enterprise-Ozark	f. Eagles
7. Faulkner State	g. Govs
8. Gadsden State	h. Lions
9. Jefferson Davis	i. Parsons
10. Jefferson State	j. Patriots
11. Lawson State	k. Pioneers
12. L.B. Wallace	l. Pirates
13. Marion Military	m. Saints
14. Shelton State	n. Sun Chiefs
15. Snead State	o. Tigers
16. Southern Union	p. Trojans
17. Wallace St. Dothan	q. Warhawks
18. Wallace St. Hanceville	r. Warhawks
19. Wallace St. Selma	s. Wildcats

The Camellia japonica was named Alabama's official State flower in 1959.

Answers

PART I

JIM NABORS SUDOKU (FROM PAGE 13)

A	J	B	O	M	S	N	I	R
M	O	I	B	N	R	J	A	S
R	N	S	A	I	J	M	B	O
N	I	R	S	B	O	A	M	J
J	S	A	M	R	N	B	O	I
B	M	O	J	A	I	S	R	N
I	B	J	R	S	M	O	N	A
S	R	M	N	O	A	I	J	B
O	A	N	I	J	B	R	S	M

TOWNES SUDOKU (FROM PAGE 13)

E	W	T	O	N	S
O	S	N	W	E	T
T	E	S	N	W	O
N	O	W	T	S	E
S	N	O	E	T	W
W	T	E	S	O	N

ACTORS CROSSWORD (FROM PAGE 14)

S	T	E	A	L		C	R	I	E	R		D	A	Y
C	O	R	G	I		R	O	D	E	O		O	N	E
A	D	O	R	N		A	L	O	N	G		P	T	A
N	O	S	E	D	I	V	E			E	P	E	E	S
			E	S	S	E		O	K	R	A			
A	D	S		E	M	S		B	I	S	E	C	T	S
T	I	P	S	Y			E	O	N		L	E	A	P
E	S	A	U		S	T	E	E	D		L	A	C	E
A	C	I	D		I	R	K			J	A	S	O	N
M	O	N	O	C	L	E		S	P	A		E	S	T
			K	A	L	E		T	I	C	S			
S	C	O	U	R			A	U	C	K	L	A	N	D
Y	I	N		T	R	A	L	A		S	O	L	E	D
N	A	Y		E	I	D	E	R		O	P	E	R	A
C	O	X		R	O	O	S	T		N	E	E	D	Y

ATHLETES CROSSWORD (FROM PAGE 20)

M	A	Y	S		H	O	U	S	E		T	A	T	S
A	B	U	T		O	F	T	E	N		H	A	R	M
R	E	L	Y		R	A	T	E	D		O	R	E	O
S	T	E	E	R	A	G	E		S	A	R	O	N	G
				A	C	E	R			R	A	N	T	S
C	A	N	A	P	E			A	P	E	X			
U	S	E	R			S	A	L	O	N		J	E	T
B	A	S	E	B	A	L	L	P	L	A	Y	E	R	S
A	P	T		R	I	A	L	S			A	R	I	A
			G	A	R	B			H	A	W	K	E	R
A	S	P	I	C			N	O	I	R				
S	H	A	R	E	S		A	R	T	P	A	P	E	R
P	A	I	D		A	D	O	B	E		S	I	L	O
E	D	G	E		C	O	M	I	C		I	N	S	T
N	E	E	D		S	M	I	T	H		A	G	E	E

STUNT DOUBLES (FROM PAGE 16)

1. LUCAS BLACK; 2. KIM DICKENS; 3. PAT BUTTRAM; 4. FELICIA DAY; 5. MARY BADHAM; 6. COURTENEY COX; 7. BARRET SWATEK; 8. MICHAEL YOUNG; 9. MICHAEL BIEHN; 10. RICHARD TYSON.

UA OR AU (FROM PAGE 19)

1. UA; 2. AU; 3. AU; 4. UA; 5. UA; 6. AU; 7. UA; 8. AU; 9. UA; 10. AU.

ALABAMA ATHLETES HODGEPODGE (FROM PAGE 22)

UA Football A-As: BENNETT, CODY, INGRAM, NAMATH, STABLER, THOMAS; Auburn Football A-As: FULLER, JACKSON, ROCKER, ROGERS, SULLIVAN; Baseball Hall of Famers: AARON, MAYS, McCOVEY, PAIGE; Auburn Basketball Stars: BARKLEY, MENGELT, PERSON; UA Basketball Stars: KING, McKEY; Olympics Champion: OWENS. Hidden Message: STEWART CINK WON THE BRITISH OPEN GOLF TOURNEY.

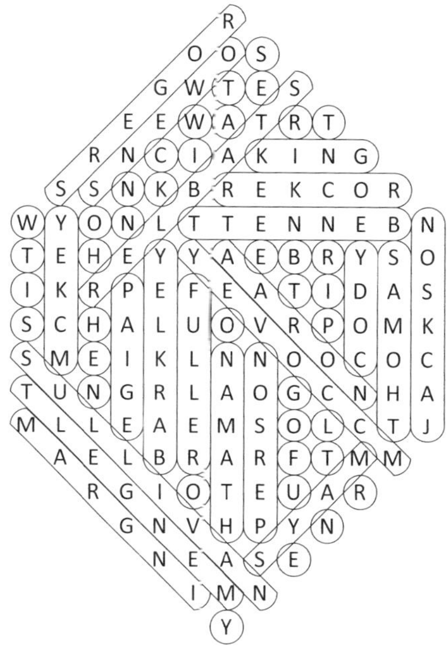

WHAT'S IN A NAME? (FROM PAGE 26)

1. j; 2. i; 3. a; 4. b; 5. d; 6. h; 7. g; 8. f; 9. c; 10. e. Bonus: DIME STORY.

TITLE BOX (FROM PAGE 27)

THE STORY OF MY LIFE.

WILSON SUDOKU (FROM PAGE 27)

N	I	W	S	O	L
O	L	S	N	I	W
W	N	I	O	L	S
L	S	O	W	N	I
I	W	N	L	S	O
S	O	L	I	W	N

AUTHORS CROSSWORD (FROM PAGE 28)

B	R	A	K	E		T	E	L		C	L	U	B	
R	E	L	A	X		O	V	A		A	O	N	E	
O	V	E	R	T		M	I	X		C	O	W	S	
			T	R	I	A	L		C	A	P	O	T	E
S	P	A		A	C	T		F	R	O		R	E	G
T	A	P	A		K	O	A	L	A		U	N	D	O
E	N	E	R	G	Y		V	E	G	A	N			
P	E	R	C	Y		L	E	E		G	R	O	O	M
			E	M	B	E	R		W	E	I	R	D	O
L	E	W	D		U	N	T	I	E		G	A	E	L
A	L	I		N	O	D		T	S	P		L	S	D
H	I	L	L	E	Y		B	A	T	E	D			
	S	L	E	W		C	O	L		T	O	U	G	H
	H	O	E	S		U	Z	I		E	S	T	E	R
	A	W	R	Y		D	O	C		R	E	E	L	S

Bama Holes (from page 32)

DON LOGAN.

Drop Down Quote (from page 33)

LADY LUCK IS INDIFFERENT. SHE SMILES SOMETIMES, AND SHE FROWNS SOMETIMES.

Industrialists Crossword (from page 34)

H	A	T	H		R	I	O	T		S	H	R	E	W
A	C	H	E		E	C	H	O		L	E	A	V	E
H	E	R	R		R	I	M	E		I	R	K	E	D
	S	U	B	D	U	E		S	O	M	B	E	R	
			R	I	N	S	E		S	E	A			
P	E	C	A	N		T	A	M	P		R	A	S	P
A	V	A	T	A	R		T	A	R		T	A	P	A
S	E	N		R	U	G		P	E	W		R	O	T
S	N	O	B		S	E	T		Y	A	H	O	O	S
E	T	N	A		T	E	A	S		F	A	N	N	Y
			T	A	I		M	I	S	E	R			
	E	T	H	I	C	S		C	A	R	B	O	N	
E	T	H	E	R		I	N	K	Y		E	L	A	N
S	C	A	R	E		L	E	E	S		R	I	T	E
T	H	I	R	D		K	E	N	O		T	O	O	T

Musicians Crossword (from page 38)

H	I	C	K	S		C	O	O	K		B	I	C	E
U	N	L	I	T		A	N	T	I		A	S	E	A
L	O	O	N	Y		P	U	T	T		S	L	A	T
A	N	T	E		P	E	S	O		P	H	A	S	E
			T	S	A	R			P	R	I	M	E	R
L	E	V	I	T	Y		T	A	L	O	N			
E	R	I	C	A		A	U	R	A		G	O	A	T
A	G	E		B	U	F	F	E	T	T		V	O	W
D	O	D	O		R	A	T	A		O	M	A	N	I
			T	E	A	R	S		O	M	E	L	E	T
P	A	S	T	E	L			A	P	E	R			
A	R	M	O	R		W	A	N	T		C	O	M	B
T	R	I	M		T	A	X	I		A	U	D	I	O
I	O	T	A		I	C	E	S		W	R	I	E	R
O	W	E	N		C	O	L	E		L	Y	N	N	E

Star Crossed (from page 40)

1. BO BICE; 2. RANDY OWEN; 3. NELL CARTER; 4. SHELBY LYNNE; 5. PERCY SLEDGE; 6. LIONEL RICHIE.

SHAW WASH (from page 41)

ASWH, HWSA, SWHA.

Alford Sudoku (from page 41)

R	D	A	O	L	F
L	F	O	R	D	A
D	R	F	A	O	L
O	A	L	F	R	D
A	L	R	D	F	O
F	O	D	L	A	R

POLITICIANS CROSSWORD (FROM PAGE 44)

A	B	L	E	■	V	A	S	E	■	B	U	S	T	S
L	I	O	N	■	A	C	I	D	■	U	T	U	R	N
O	B	O	E	■	M	O	L	E	■	S	E	P	I	A
E	L	M	■	C	O	R	O	N	A	■	■	R	A	F
S	E	S	S	I	O	N	S	■	X	A	N	A	D	U
■	■	■	I	T	S				I	R	A	■	■	■
B	Y	E	B	Y	E				S	T	Y	L	U	S
R	O	T	■	■	■				■	■	■	E	R	A
A	N	C	H	O	R				R	A	T	I	N	G
■	■	■	A	D	O				E	G	O	■	■	■
N	A	U	S	E	A	■	U	S	S	E	N	A	T	E
I	L	L	■	■	D	O	T	T	E	D	■	G	O	V
N	I	T	T	Y	■	S	T	U	N	■	N	I	N	A
E	E	R	I	E	■	L	E	N	D	■	B	L	E	D
S	N	A	P	S	■	O	R	T	S	■	C	E	D	E

ALABAMA GOVERNORS WORD SEARCH (FROM PAGE 46)

N	E	S	C	O	L	E	W	I	S	Y	J	M	C	L
U	E	H	N	O	T	T	A	P	W	A	T	T	S	R
T	E	Y	U	S	B	I	L	C	J	E	D	M	H	S
N	R	E	W	E	R	B	L	N	J	S	I	I	M	Y
U	O	L	I	N	D	S	A	Y	O	T	X	B	I	Z
H	O	S	R	O	L	M	C	S	H	D	O	M	L	O
L	M	A	R	J	L	L	E	Y	N	H	N	L	L	K
G	Y	E	H	E	N	D	E	R	S	O	N	A	E	I
P	E	B	G	A	T	L	E	W	T	N	S	D	R	L
M	L	E	U	G	T	T	T	U	O	W	E	R	X	B
O	I	P	G	N	R	J	A	T	N	D	H	O	E	Y
S	R	K	E	O	E	A	S	P	B	Y	C	F	W	P
L	P	B	H	L	M	U	V	K	J	J	A	M	E	S
O	T	S	K	W	O	A	T	E	S	K	R	A	P	S
F	O	S	K	H	C	P	A	R	S	O	N	S	A	M

BUILD THE NAMES (FROM PAGE 47)

1. SESSIONS; 2. BANKHEAD; 3. SPARKMAN; 4. DENTON; 5. HEFLIN; 6. MORGAN; 7. STEWART; 8. SHELBY.

CRYPTIC QUOTE (FROM PAGE 52)

"I CAN BE A VOICE IN THE MOVEMENT TO IMPROVE OUR NATION'S HEALTH CARE AND OUR NATION'S HEALTH. I WANT TO BE SURE THAT NO ONE FALLS THROUGH THE CRACKS AS WE IMPROVE OUR HEALTH CARE SYSTEM."

WOMEN CROSSWORD (FROM PAGE 50)

G	L	A	D	■	A	S	I	F	■	A	G	A	P	E
R	I	C	E	■	M	I	L	L	■	A	L	L	E	N
A	N	T	E	■	A	X	L	E	■	H	A	T	E	D
D	E	S	P	O	T	■	S	A	P	■	S	O	N	S
■	■	■	S	P	I	T	■	■	I	T	S	■	■	■
P	O	P	E	S	■	H	A	R	S	H	■	M	O	D
A	R	E	A	■	D	E	L	E	T	E	■	O	N	O
R	I	O	■	J	E	M	I	S	O	N	■	C	A	W
K	E	N	■	U	N	E	V	E	N	■	T	H	I	N
S	L	Y	■	M	O	D	E	L	■	B	E	A	R	S
■	■	■	O	P	T	■	■	L	I	R	A	■	■	■
B	O	W	L	■	E	L	K	■	D	O	C	K	E	D
E	R	O	D	E	■	O	N	T	O	■	A	N	T	I
D	A	V	I	S	■	C	O	A	L	■	K	I	N	G
S	L	E	E	P	■	I	B	I	S	■	E	T	A	S

WHO AM I? SUDOKU (FROM PAGE 53)

Mahala Ashley DICKERSON.

N	K	O	C	S	I	E	D	R
I	C	E	N	R	D	K	S	O
R	S	D	E	O	K	C	N	I
K	O	N	S	I	C	D	R	E
D	I	C	K	E	R	S	O	N
E	R	S	D	N	O	I	C	K
O	E	K	R	C	S	N	I	D
C	N	I	O	D	E	R	K	S
S	D	R	I	K	N	O	E	C

WALKER SUDOKU (FROM PAGE 53)

W	E	L	K	A	R
K	A	R	W	E	L
R	L	A	E	K	W
E	K	W	R	L	A
L	W	E	A	R	K
A	R	K	L	W	E

OTHERS CROSSWORD (FROM PAGE 56)

S	E	E	P	■	S	H	A	D	E	■	S	T	E	P
C	A	V	E	■	H	U	M	A	N	■	C	U	R	E
U	S	E	R	■	A	M	E	B	A	■	O	T	I	S
B	E	N	J	A	M	I	N	■	B	L	O	U	N	T
A	S	S	U	R	E	D	■	S	L	I	P	■	■	■
■	■	■	R	E	D	■	G	A	I	N	■	A	S	H
T	R	A	Y	■	■	D	R	U	N	K	■	L	E	E
H	I	M	■	P	A	R	I	N	G	S	■	T	A	R
A	L	I	■	L	L	A	M	A	■	■	T	O	M	B
W	E	D	■	E	S	P	Y	■	P	T	A	■	■	■
■	■	■	O	B	O	E	■	F	A	U	X	P	A	S
C	A	R	V	E	R	■	V	O	N	B	R	A	U	N
A	R	E	A	■	A	F	I	R	E	■	A	G	R	A
L	I	A	R	■	N	A	S	A	L	■	T	E	A	R
L	A	D	Y	■	S	T	A	Y	S	■	E	R	S	E

SHE SAID WHAT? (FROM PAGE 58)

"I WAS BORN IN ALABAMA, BUT I ONLY LIVED THERE FOR A MONTH BEFORE I'D DONE EVERYTHING THERE WAS TO DO."

TXT NAMES (FROM PAGE 59)

1. Condoleezza RICE; 2. Robert GIBBS; 3. Deidre DOWNS; 4. Timothy LEARY; 5. Jimmy WALES; 6. Mel ALLEN; 7. Tom JOYNER; 8. Mae Carol JEMISON.

PART II

NORTHWEST CROSSWORD (FROM PAGE 64)

■	J	E	R	K	■	C	H	I	C	■	S	H	E	■
■	O	V	E	N	■	H	A	M	I	L	T	O	N	■
■	H	I	V	E	■	I	M	P	A	I	R	E	D	■
A	N	D	■	E	E	L	■	■	■	M	A	D	■	■
I	D	E	A	■	K	I	D	■	C	O	Y	O	T	E
M	O	N	R	O	E	■	E	V	E	■	S	W	A	B
S	E	T	T	O	■	■	A	I	D	E	■	N	U	B
■	■	■	S	H	E	F	F	I	E	L	D	■	■	■
E	R	R	■	S	L	O	E	■	■	S	I	R	E	N
R	E	E	D	■	K	E	N	■	A	E	R	A	T	E
E	X	C	E	S	S	■	S	A	Y	■	E	T	A	S
■	■	Y	A	P	■	■	■	G	E	L	■	H	I	T
■	O	C	C	A	S	I	O	N	■	I	D	O	L	■
■	F	L	O	R	E	N	C	E	■	M	U	L	E	■
■	T	E	N	■	A	N	T	S	■	P	E	E	R	■

NORTHWEST WORD SEARCH (FROM PAGE 67)

Q	V	K	I	L	L	E	N	O	S	I	D	D	A	V
V	H	O	D	G	E	S	G	R	U	B	W	E	N	L
T	H	G	I	R	W	L	W	I	N	F	I	E	L	D
Y	E	L	R	A	N	A	F	O	C	N	I	G	L	E
F	N	Z	E	A	N	O	T	L	I	M	A	H	E	D
M	I	D	W	A	Y	H	T	X	O	I	S	K	B	K
H	W	H	N	V	G	S	B	T	B	R	H	R	S	N
A	T	N	I	I	Z	E	O	M	A	T	E	D	I	A
L	Y	N	E	L	L	L	U	N	D	H	F	N	J	B
L	A	L	I	G	L	C	W	R	E	N	F	A	C	D
T	B	C	R	U	S	S	E	L	L	V	I	L	L	E
O	D	E	K	U	G	U	B	E	M	W	E	E	W	R
W	E	S	T	O	N	M	B	O	A	A	L	R	I	B
N	R	D	O	O	W	K	C	O	R	C	D	O	B	N
B	A	R	T	O	N	O	T	L	U	O	M	M	P	X

NORTHWEST FIND THE WORDS (FROM PAGE 66)

DEELY, DEERS, DELES, DESSE, DYERS, ELDER, ELDERS, ENDER, ENDERS, ENDEW, ENDEWS, ENDWISE, EYEDNESS, EYELESS, EYERS, LEERS, LENDER, LENDERS, LENDS, LESES, LESSER, LYSED, NEEDLE, NEEDLES, NEEDLY, NEEDS, NEEDY, PIEDNESS, PIERS, REDELESS, REDES, REDLY, REDNESS, REDYE, REDYES,REEDE, REEDES, REEDS, REEDY, REELED, RESEND, SEDER, SEDERS, SEDES, SEEDS, SEEDY, SEELD, SEELED, SEELY, SEERS, SEIRS, SELDSEEN, SELES, SENDER, SENDERS, SIELD, SIRED, SIREE, SIREES, SIRES, SPIED, SPIEL, SPIELED, SPIER, SPIERS, SPIES, SPIRE, SPIRED, SPIRES, SPIREWISE, SWEDE, SWEDES, SWEED, SWEEL, SWEELED, SWEES, SWEIR, SWEIRS, SWEYED, SWEYS, SWIES, SWIPIER, SWIRE, SWIRES, WEDEL, WEDELN,WEEDS, WEEDY, WEIRS, WIELD, WIELDER, WIELDERS, WIELDS, WIELDY, WIRED, WIRES, WISED, WISELY, WISPY, WRIED, WRIES, WYLED, WYLES, YEDES, YEEDS, YESSED, YIELD, YIELDER, YIELDERS, YIELDS.

BAMA BUILDING BLOCKS (FROM PAGE 70)

1. ROGERS; 2. OGRES; 3. GORE; 4. ORE; 5. OR; 6. O.

DECATUR WORDSMITH (FROM PAGE 71)

ACED, ACRE, ACRED, ACTED, ACUTE, ACUTER, ARCED, CADE, CADET, CADRE, CARD, CARE, CARED, CARET, CART, CARTE, CARTED, CATE, CATER, CEDAR, CRATE, CRATED, CRED, CRUD, CRUDE, CRUET, CUED, CURATE, CURATED, CURD, CURE, CURED, CURET, CURT, CUTE, CUTER, DACE, DARE, DART, DATE, DATER, DAUT, DEAR, DERAT, DRAT, DUCAT, DUCE, DUCT, DUET, DURA, DURE, ECRU, EDUCT, ERUCT, RACE, RACED, RATE, RATED, REACT, READ, RECTA, RECUT, REDACT, RUDE, RUED, TACE, TARE, TARED, TEAR, TRACE, TRACED, TRAD, TRADE, TRADUCE, TREAD, TRUCE, TRUCED, TRUE, TRUED, TURD, URATE, UREA.

NORTHEAST CROSSWORD (FROM PAGE 72)

O	H	I	O	■	G	O	N	G	■	S	C	A	N	T
P	E	N	N	■	O	P	A	L	■	H	U	R	O	N
S	I	T	E	■	R	E	N	O	■	A	L	I	S	T
■	R	O	O	F	E	R	■	P	A	R	L	A	Y	■
■	■	■	N	A	S	A	■	■	D	I	M	■	■	■
S	P	I	T	Z	■	S	A	R	I	■	A	C	E	S
U	L	N	A	E	■	■	D	U	E	■	N	A	A	N
S	E	A	■	D	E	C	A	T	U	R	■	P	S	I
H	A	N	G	■	L	O	P	■	■	O	A	R	E	D
I	D	E	A	■	I	O	T	A	■	U	T	I	L	E
■	■	■	D	O	T	■	■	D	E	N	T	■	■	■
■	C	A	S	P	E	R	■	U	P	D	A	T	E	■
P	A	N	D	A	■	A	B	L	E	■	L	E	A	D
A	P	T	E	R	■	M	O	T	E	■	L	A	S	E
P	O	I	N	T	■	P	A	S	S	■	A	M	E	N

BAILEYTON SUDOKU (FROM PAGE 74)

L	I	Y	B	T	O	N	A	E
E	B	A	I	N	L	Y	T	O
O	T	N	A	Y	E	L	I	B
N	Y	T	E	O	I	A	B	L
I	E	B	L	A	N	T	O	Y
A	O	L	Y	B	T	I	E	N
B	L	I	N	E	A	O	Y	T
Y	N	O	T	I	B	E	L	A
T	A	E	O	L	Y	B	N	I

MISSING H-A-L-E (FROM PAGE 77)

1. HAILED; 2. BEHALF; 3. HERBAL; 4. HEALTH; 5. WEALTH; 6. LATHER; 7. HALVES; 8. CHALET; 9. AWHILE; 10. HASSLE; 11. WHALES; 12. BLEACH. Bonus: EXHALE, INHALE.

HIGDON SUDOKU (FROM PAGE 74)

D	H	O	N	G	I
N	I	G	O	H	D
H	O	I	G	D	N
G	D	N	I	O	H
O	N	H	D	I	G
I	G	D	H	N	O

CENTRAL WEST FILL-IN (FROM PAGE 78)

		S				M	I	L	L	P	O	R	T	
F		T				E				R				
E		A		C		M			Y	O	R	K		
R	A	N	D	O	L	P	H			S		E		S
N		S		A		H				P		N		I
B	R	E	N	T		I				E		N		P
A		L		O		S				C	R	E	W	S
N				P				A		T		D		E
K	A	N	S	A	S			S				Y		Y
					A			H		E			B	
F	O	S	T	E	R	S		B	O	L	I	G	E	E
					A			Y		D			L	
	M		G		G					R			M	
	C		O		O			C	L	I	N	T	O	N
	S		R		S					D			N	
	H		D		S	U	L	L	I	G	E	N	T	
P	A	N	O	L	A		A			E				E
	N						W							C
					R	A	L	P	H		W			H
E	M	P	I	R	E		E		A		A			O
L					F		Y		M	A	R	V	E	L
R		A	K	R	O	N			N		S			A
O					R		S	T	E	W	A	R	T	
D					M				R		W			

CENTRAL WEST CROSSWORD (FROM PAGE 80)

S	T	E	M		L	U	T	I	S	T		B	R	A
T	A	M	E		A	Z	A	L	E	A		R	O	D
Y	O	U	R	E	D	I	X	I	E	S		O	B	I
			I	C	Y			A	R	K		T	E	E
S	L	O	T	H		I	T	D			T	H	R	U
E	O	N		O	D	O	R		H	E	I	S	T	
W	A	T	T		E	W	E		I	R	E			
	F	O	O	T	B	A	L	L	P	R	I	D	E	
			R	O	T		L	O	T		N	O	V	A
	T	A	C	O	S		I	D	O	L		N	I	P
D	I	S	H			U	S	E		E	A	G	L	E
E	T	C		S	O	N			P	A	C			
L	I	E		C	R	I	M	S	O	N	T	I	D	E
T	A	N		A	C	T	O	U	T		O	V	E	N
A	N	D		M	A	Y	A	N	S		R	E	N	D

CENTRAL EAST CROSSWORD (FROM PAGE 84)

T	U	T	U		R	E	S		A	L	P	I	N	E
A	K	I	N		O	V	A		T	I	E	D	Y	E
B	E	S	S	E	M	E	R		O	C	L	O	C	K
			A	L	E		C	A	M	E	L			
B	L	U	F	F		S	A	G	S		C	A	I	N
E	A	S	E		A	L	S	O		M	I	C	R	O
D	Y	E		T	R	I	M		S	E	T	T	E	R
			A	H	E	M		M	A	N	Y			
B	O	S	N	I	A		O	U	R	S		A	W	E
I	R	O	N	S		H	I	F	I		C	L	O	T
D	E	L	I		G	O	L	F		P	O	L	K	A
			S	N	E	E	R		C	A	N			
B	E	A	T	E	N		I	R	O	N	D	A	L	E
A	F	L	O	A	T		G	Y	M		O	V	E	R
S	T	I	N	T	S		S	E	A		S	E	E	R

Malone Sudoku
(from page 86)

L	E	M	N	O	A
N	O	A	L	E	M
M	L	E	A	N	O
A	N	O	E	M	L
O	A	N	M	L	E
E	M	L	O	A	N

Muscadine Sudoku
(from page 86)

C	D	M	S	I	N	U	E	A
S	I	E	U	C	A	M	N	D
A	U	N	D	E	M	I	S	C
N	A	D	I	U	E	S	C	M
M	S	U	A	N	C	D	I	E
I	E	C	M	D	S	A	U	N
E	M	A	C	S	U	N	D	I
U	N	I	E	A	D	C	M	S
D	C	S	N	M	I	E	A	U

Central East Word Search
(from page 87)

M	A	H	A	R	G	O	I	S	I	C	L	A	C	M
A	L	M	O	N	D	O	O	W	E	M	O	H	A	U
H	Y	P	K	E	L	A	D	N	O	R	I	I	L	N
L	B	D	E	L	A	D	N	O	T	L	U	F	E	Y
E	L	L	E	L	A	D	N	E	D	R	A	G	R	B
P	E	E	K	I	L	A	G	E	D	A	L	L	A	T
I	H	I	U	V	U	C	R	E	B	N	X	N	B	L
N	S	F	D	S	K	S	I	E	R	N	W	E	D	I
S	A	R	Y	S	B	W	L	T	D	I	S	O	N	N
O	Y	A	G	U	A	C	A	L	Y	S	Y	R	A	C
N	R	B	R	R	K	L	V	H	E	T	D	F	L	O
A	E	G	L	T	A	B	P	M	N	O	O	N	G	L
D	E	T	N	O	M	D	E	I	P	N	O	E	A	N
O	X	F	O	R	D	R	O	F	N	U	M	R	R	B
S	N	I	L	L	O	H	A	T	L	E	D	J	T	Y

Mideast Crossword
(from page 90)

S	P	O	T	■	V	I	L	E	R	■	O	P	A	L
H	E	R	O	■	E	V	O	K	E	■	P	E	S	O
O	R	E	O	■	G	I	B	E	D	■	E	R	I	N
T	U	S	K	E	G	E	E	■	■	S	L	I	D	E
■	■	■	A	R	I	D	■	S	P	O	I	L	E	R
I	N	L	I	N	E	■	T	H	I	N	K	■	■	■
M	A	I	M	S	■	E	R	A	S	■	A	L	B	S
P	R	O	■	T	U	B	U	L	A	R	■	I	R	A
S	Y	N	C	■	P	O	S	T	■	I	B	E	A	M
■	■	■	L	O	O	N	S	■	O	N	E	D	G	E
S	C	R	A	W	N	Y	■	N	A	S	A	■	■	■
T	H	I	N	E	■	■	P	I	K	E	R	O	A	D
R	A	F	T	■	S	T	E	E	L	■	C	A	S	E
O	S	L	O	■	P	E	A	C	E	■	A	R	E	A
P	E	E	N	■	A	L	L	E	Y	■	T	S	A	R

Opelika Wordsmith (from page 92)

ALIKE, ALKIE, ALOE, ILEA, ILKA, KAIL, KALE, KELP, KEPI, KILO, KOEL, KOLA, LAKE, LEAK, LEAP, LIKE, LIPA, LIPE, LOPE, OKAPI, OLEA, OPAL, PAIK, PAIL, PALE, PEAK, PEAL, PIAL, PIKA, PIKE, PILE, PILEA, PLEA, PLIE, POKE, POLE, POLKA.

MADE IN MOBILE (FROM PAGE 96)

1. e; 2. f; 3. g; 4. b; 5. d; 6. a; 7. j; 8. h; 9. i; 10. c.

GULF COAST IF . . . THEN (FROM PAGE 97)

SENIOR BOWL.

ONE AND ONLY ONE ROBA (FROM PAGE 93)

R	B	O	A	O	R	R	B	A	O	R	O	B	O	R
O	B	A	R	B	O	A	R	O	B	B	O	R	A	O
B	A	O	R	O	A	B	O	O	B	R	O	B	R	B
R	O	B	B	A	O	R	B	B	A	R	A	B	R	O
R	O	B	B	R	R	O	B	O	R	B	O	R	B	A
O	B	A	R	O	B	O	B	A	R	O	B	B	A	O
R	B	O	A	A	A	B	B	B	O	O	O	R	R	R
O	R	B	A	R	B	B	O	O	R	O	O	B	O	O
B	O	O	R	B	A	R	B	O	A	B	R	A	B	R
O	R	B	A	B	O	B	A	A	A	B	O	A	O	A
R	A	B	A	B	B	O	A	A	R	B	O	O	B	R
O	A	B	B	A	R	R	A	O	O	B	A	B	O	B
B	R	O	R	R	A	R	R	A	R	O	R	O	A	O
R	A	B	O	O	R	B	A	O	R	R	B	A	R	O
O	R	O	A	O	B	A	O	B	A	O	R	B	O	R

GULF COAST CROSSWORD (FROM PAGE 98)

		T	U	B		R	A	N	G		A	N	O	N
	G	U	R	U		O	D	O	R		D	A	F	T
S	O	N	N	Y		L	E	G	O		M	Y	T	H
N	U	N	S		A	L	P		O	V	A			
O	D	E		S	C	O	T		M	O	N	R	O	E
B	A	L	D	W	I	N		F	E	W		E	R	A
			D	U	D		C	A	D		T	E	A	S
M	A	D	A	M		B	O	Y		H	I	L	L	Y
A	W	A	Y		S	A	Y		M	U	M			
R	O	T		S	P	Y		M	A	R	E	N	G	O
C	L	A	R	K	E		C	E	N	T		Y	A	P
			O	I	L		O	N	E		B	L	U	E
A	V	E	S		L	E	N	T		B	L	O	N	D
K	I	W	I		E	R	G	O		A	U	N	T	
A	M	E	N		R	E	A	R		H	R	S		

BUTLER SUDOKU (FROM PAGE 100)

U	R	L	T	E	B
E	T	B	R	U	L
B	E	R	L	T	U
T	L	U	B	R	E
R	B	E	U	L	T
L	U	T	E	B	R

GULF CREST SUDOKU (FROM PAGE 100)

R	F	E	S	C	G	U	T	L
G	L	C	T	U	F	S	E	R
T	U	S	R	E	L	G	C	F
U	S	T	L	G	C	F	R	E
L	E	G	F	T	R	C	S	U
C	R	F	U	S	E	T	L	G
F	T	U	E	R	S	L	G	C
S	C	R	G	L	U	E	F	T
E	G	L	C	F	T	R	U	S

SOUTHEAST CROSSWORD (FROM PAGE 104)

I	N	C	H		M	U	F	F			D	I	S	H
D	A	R	E		A	S	E	A		R	O	D	E	O
E	V	E	R	G	R	E	E	N		A	T	E	A	M
S	E	W		L	I	F	T		I	N	H	A	L	E
			L	I	E	U		S	T	E	A	L	S	
S	W	E	A	T		L	O	O	S	E	N			
P	I	A	Z	Z	A		C	U	E			F	B	I
A	R	T	Y		S	W	E	L	L		P	I	E	D
Y	E	S			S	E	A		F	L	O	R	A	L
			A	D	O	R	N	S		Y	U	M	M	Y
	M	A	T	U	R	E		U	S	S	R			
H	E	L	M	E	T		I	N	T	O		A	S	P
I	D	I	O	T		A	N	D	A	L	U	S	I	A
T	I	E	R	S		A	F	A	R		S	A	N	G
S	A	N	E			H	O	E	R		A	P	S	E

SOUTHEAST WORD SEARCH (FROM PAGE 106)

U	C	H	E	E	U	F	A	U	L	A	V	O	N	R
R	E	I	Z	O	D	U	K	I	N	S	E	Y	J	N
B	H	N	A	I	S	U	L	A	D	N	A	D	O	E
L	S	T	T	A	R	P	I	A	T	E	N	O	N	Q
A	W	P	K	E	E	G	O	B	R	E	W	T	O	N
C	E	E	H	U	R	T	S	B	O	R	O	H	T	P
K	U	Z	L	O	P	P	S	E	Y	G	C	A	Y	S
N	X	E	E	L	E	Q	R	V	T	R	V	N	A	K
P	S	G	Y	T	I	C	X	I	N	E	H	P	L	O
H	P	E	N	R	E	V	U	L	S	V	E	O	C	O
A	E	M	A	R	L	F	N	L	G	E	O	Z	B	R
C	R	N	O	L	R	O	Y	E	L	T	N	A	R	B
O	O	M	C	K	E	N	Z	I	E	O	Z	R	Y	E
D	T	X	C	M	A	S	H	F	O	R	D	K	R	C
A	E	D	W	I	N	L	J	L	X	C	G	X	Q	K

COMPLETE THE 'VILLES (FROM PAGE 103)

1. FREEMANVILLE; 2. DIXONVILLE; 3. JOHNSONVILLE; 4. GREENVILLE; 5. LIBERTYVILLE; 6. LOUISVILLE; 7. SKIPPERVILLE; 8. LAWRENCEVILLE.

PART III

ARTS & ENTERTAINMENT CROSSWORD (FROM PAGE 110)

R	I	B		S	P	A	S	M		S	M	O	K	E
E	M	U		O	R	A	T	E		H	A	L	E	Y
A	P	T		D	O	R	I	S		R	I	D	G	E
C	O	L	L	A	B	O	R	A	T	I	N	G		
T	R	E	E		E	N	S		O	M	E	L	E	T
S	T	R	A	W				S	U	P		O	R	E
			D	A	B		B	O	P			R	I	D
M	O	M		S	O	F	A	B	E	D		Y	E	S
A	L	I			N	O	R		E	A	T			
R	I	G		U	S	E				M	O	T	I	F
C	O	R	O	N	A		S	U	B		N	I	N	A
		A	R	T	I	S	T	P	R	O	G	R	A	M
A	M	I	G	O		T	A	P	I	R		A	N	I
C	A	N	A	L		E	R	E	C	T		D	E	N
T	R	E	N	D		P	E	R	K	S		E	R	E

BUSINESS CROSSWORD (FROM PAGE 116)

H	U	M	S		A	S	P	I	C		A	L	I	T
E	T	A	L		S	T	A	L	L		N	O	D	E
S	A	G	A		T	E	S	L	A		D	U	E	L
	H	I	B	B	E	R	T	S	P	O	R	T	S	
				A	R	E			S	U	E			
L	O	Y	A	L		O	D	E		T	A	S	K	S
A	V	E	R	S	E		I	S	M			T	A	I
V	U	L	C	A	N	M	A	T	E	R	I	A	L	S
E	L	L			D	U	N		W	E	D	G	E	S
R	E	S	E	W		M	A	R		B	O	S	S	Y
			M	O	P				A	G	E			
	B	O	O	K	S	A	M	I	L	L	I	O	N	
C	O	R	N		A	R	I	S	E		T	I	E	R
V	I	C	E		L	E	N	I	N		E	L	A	N
S	L	A	Y		M	A	I	N	S		M	Y	R	A

HARDIN SUDOKU (FROM PAGE 112)

H	I	A	N	D	R
D	R	N	H	I	A
I	H	R	A	N	D
N	A	D	R	H	I
A	D	H	I	R	N
R	N	I	D	A	H

PLAYHOUSE SUDOKU (FROM PAGE 112)

U	H	S	L	Y	P	O	E	A
L	Y	E	O	U	A	S	P	H
A	O	P	H	E	S	Y	L	U
P	A	H	Y	O	E	L	U	S
S	L	O	A	P	U	H	Y	E
Y	E	U	S	H	L	A	O	P
E	S	A	U	L	O	P	H	Y
O	P	Y	E	A	H	U	S	L
H	U	L	P	S	Y	E	A	O

FRAMED ARTISTS (FROM PAGE 113)

1. HOVENDEN; 2. LAWRENCE; 3. REYNOLDS; 4. WHEATLEY; 5. GERHARDT; 6. BRIDGMAN.

BOEING SUDOKU (FROM PAGE 118)

B	I	G	O	N	E
E	O	N	B	G	I
G	E	I	N	O	B
O	N	B	I	E	G
I	G	O	E	B	N
N	B	E	G	I	O

BRASFIELD SUDOKU (FROM PAGE 118)

R	E	L	F	S	B	A	I	D
F	A	S	I	L	D	R	E	B
I	D	E	R	B	S	L	A	F
B	S	R	E	F	I	D	L	A
S	L	F	D	A	R	I	B	E
E	B	I	A	D	L	S	F	R
A	F	D	L	I	E	B	R	S
L	R	B	S	E	A	F	D	I
D	I	A	B	R	F	E	S	L

CROSSWORD CONSTRUCTOR (FROM PAGE 119)

P	E	P
I	R	E
E	R	A

C	A	T
A	L	A
R	E	P

EDUCATION CROSSWORD (FROM PAGE 122)

P	I	N	O	T		G	A	L	E		C	H	A	R
S	N	A	F	U		O	M	E	N		H	A	V	E
S	T	A	T	S		O	P	A	L		A	L	E	E
T	O	N		K	I	D		S	A	M	F	O	R	D
			D	E	B	S			R	O	E			
	R	O	U	G	E		M	E	G	A		P	T	A
V	O	R	T	E	X		I	R	E		P	R	I	G
A	P	A	C	E		A	L	E		S	L	I	M	E
M	E	T	H		O	R	E		E	T	U	D	E	S
P	R	E		T	O	M	S		T	I	N	E	S	
			O	W	L			S	U	L	K			
O	A	K	W	O	O	D		N	I	L		I	T	S
A	M	E	N		N	O	V	A		M	U	R	A	L
H	O	N	E		G	L	O	P		A	F	I	R	E
U	S	S	R		S	E	W	S		N	O	S	E	D

COLLEGES WORD SEARCH (FROM PAGE 124)

L	Y	M	H	F	F	S	A	M	F	O	R	D	N	M
X	O	E	U	O	A	K	W	O	O	D	D	L	D	O
S	R	T	N	E	U	A	I	N	I	G	R	I	V	B
E	T	A	T	S	L	L	I	V	E	B	E	M	V	I
L	S	T	I	E	K	A	X	F	T	T	I	M	Y	L
I	P	S	N	T	N	B	T	S	A	A	D	O	T	E
M	R	P	G	A	E	A	U	T	T	L	S	N	N	F
S	I	O	D	T	R	M	S	I	S	L	T	T	O	G
E	N	H	O	S	A	A	K	L	S	A	A	E	S	D
G	G	S	N	D	M	A	E	L	N	D	T	V	D	A
D	H	I	N	A	L	&	G	M	E	E	E	A	U	U
I	I	B	B	E	E	M	E	A	H	G	S	L	J	B
R	L	A	Y	N	S	O	E	N	T	A	K	L	Q	U
M	L	A	W	S	O	N	S	T	A	T	E	O	V	R
A	I	D	R	O	C	N	O	C	A	L	H	O	U	N

WHERE ARE THEY? (FROM PAGE 125)

1. h; 2. i; 3. f; 4. b; 5. d; 6. a; 7. j; 8. c; 9. g; 10. e.

ALABAMA TIME LINE (FROM PAGE 130)

1. b; 2. d; 3. j; 4. g; 5. c; 6. f; 7. a; 8. h; 9. e; 10. i.

ALABAMA CITIES FROM A TO Z (FROM PAGE 131)

ALMA, BABBIE, CECIL, DIAMOND, ELMORE, FYFFE, GEIGER, HEATH, IRVINGTON, JOPPA, KIRK, LILLIAN, MEMPHIS, NEWTON, ORION, PROSPECT, QUINTON, RAMER, SILAS, TITUS, UNITY, VANDIVER, WARSAW, EXCEL, YANTLEY, ZIP CITY.

History Crossword (from page 128)

P	L	O	D	■	W	H	I	T	E	■	P	L	A	Y
L	I	V	E	■	E	A	V	E	S	■	R	O	V	E
O	R	A	L	■	B	R	E	N	T	■	I	C	O	N
W	A	L	L	A	C	E	■	P	A	R	S	O	N	S
■	■	■	S	H	A	M	■	I	T	E	M	■	■	■
O	P	T	■	E	M	S	■	N	E	T	■	L	O	W
C	L	A	I	M						D	E	A	T	H
E	U	R	O	■						■	M	U	T	E
A	T	O	N	E						S	U	R	E	R
N	O	T	■	D	A	M	■	D	E	W	■	A	R	E
■	■	■	S	I	Z	E	■	E	L	A	N	■	■	■
C	H	O	C	T	A	W	■	M	O	N	A	R	C	H
L	A	M	A	■	L	I	T	U	P	■	K	A	Y	O
U	R	A	L	■	E	N	U	R	E	■	E	T	A	L
B	E	N	D	■	A	G	N	E	S	■	D	E	N	Y

Recreation Crossword (from page 134)

O	B	E	S	E	■	O	D	D	■	■	T	I	T	O
W	A	L	E	S	■	P	A	D	■	R	O	T	O	R
L	A	K	E	P	O	I	N	T	■	A	S	S	E	T
■	■	■	D	R	U	N	K	■	C	V	S	■	■	■
T	S	P	■	I	R	E	■	P	H	I	■	S	P	A
H	E	A	R	T	S	■	O	R	E	O	■	T	U	G
Y	A	R	N	■	■	K	N	E	E	L	■	I	L	O
■	B	L	A	D	O	N	S	P	R	I	N	G	S	■
B	I	O	■	O	G	E	E	S	■	■	I	M	A	M
O	R	R	■	B	R	A	T	■	R	E	L	A	T	E
A	D	S	■	B	E	D	■	R	E	V	■	S	E	T
■	■	■	G	I	S	■	P	A	N	I	C	■	■	■
B	E	G	I	N	■	W	I	N	D	C	R	E	E	K
B	R	A	G	S	■	E	T	C	■	T	O	R	T	E
C	A	D	S	■	■	B	A	H	■	S	P	R	A	Y

State Parks Word Search (from page 136)

Z
W B Y
N I C E U
Q O N R L O O
H A S D Z E C U V
K C I K H
E C R S A A A
L J A E G L T R E
H A Q J E N B T O N M
P K K I Y A L
G C N E R V H A N
Q Z H A V P X O N I H
S G N I R P S N O D A L B
A C F E E E C C T
A L K C O U E H O N S
P L C A H N L L E O U W Q
N U A A S E A B R E P O Y Z Y
R W A A S D U C E M S
J O E W H E E L E R K I M
Z B L H W A T S E A X A U S H
G U L F C C Q N O K H K O P B G K
O T A
M O L
U R X

Sports Crossword (from page 140)

M	A	L	L	■	S	O	L	I	D	■	T	A	R	■
A	L	O	E	■	T	R	O	V	E	■	H	I	E	■
M	O	B	I	L	E	B	A	Y	B	E	A	R	S	■
A	T	E	■	E	R	I	N	■	■	N	I	E	C	E
■	■	■	C	E	N	T	■	Y	A	M	■	R	U	T
A	C	T	O	R	S	■	R	I	C	E	■	S	E	A
A	P	E	S	■	■	T	E	E	N	S	Y	■	■	■
H	U	N	T	S	V	I	L	L	E	H	A	V	O	C
■	■	■	S	U	I	T	E	D	■	■	C	I	A	O
I	T	S	■	B	E	L	T	■	T	S	H	I	R	T
R	O	C	■	U	S	E	■	T	I	L	T	■	■	■
A	B	H	O	R	■	■	Y	E	T	I	■	V	E	T
■	A	L	A	B	A	M	A	H	A	M	M	E	R	S
■	G	E	T	■	L	O	R	E	N	■	A	R	I	A
■	O	P	S	■	L	O	D	E	S	■	D	Y	E	R

Across & Down Words (from page 137)

Across: SWIM, CAMP, SAIL, GOLF, FISH, HUNT; Down: HIKING, JETSKI, MUSEUM, PICNIC; Place: LAKEPOINT RESORT STATE PARK.

What is It? (from page 142)

1. FIRST DOWN; 2. INCOMPLETE PASS; 3. LITTLE LEAGUE; 4. POP UP; 5. THREE-POINTERS; 6. DOUBLE DRIBBLE; 7. BLUE LINE; 8. BREAKAWAY.

Mascot Match (from page 143)

1. f; 2. s; 3. q or r; 4. p; 5. l; 6. b; 7. n; 8. d; 9. q or r; 10. k; 11. e; 12. m; 13. o; 14. c; 15. i; 16. a; 17. g; 18. h; 19. j.

Bibliography

For more information about the great state of Alabama, check out these books and Websites:

Books:

AAA. 2012. *Alabama & Florida Panhandle Tour Book*. AAA Publishing.

Duncan, Andy. 2009. *Alabama Curiosities, 2nd: Characters, Roadside Oddities & Other Offbeat Stuff*. Globe Pequot.

Martin, Gay N. 2009. *Alabama Off the Beaten Path, 9th: A Guide to Unique Places*. GPP Travel.

Van Der Veer Hamilton, Virginia. 1984. *Alabam*a. W.W. Norton and Company, Inc.

Wilkerson, Lyn. 2010. *Slow Travels—Alabama*. Lulu.com.

Websites:

People

http://en.wikipedia.org/wiki/List_of_people_from_Alabama

http://www.thingstodo.com/states/AL/famous_people.htm

Places

http://en.wikipedia.org/wiki/List_of_places_in_Alabama

http://www.alabama.travel/

Activities

http://www.al.com/events/things-to-do/

http://attractions.uptake.com/alabama.html